COMMUNICATIONS
at SEA

COMMUNICATIONS
at SEA

MIKE HARRIS

SHERIDAN HOUSE

This edition first published 2003
In the United States of America
by Sheridan House Inc.
145 Palisade Street
Dobbs Ferry, NY 10522
www.sheridanhouse.com

A CIP catalog record for this book is available from
the Library of Congress, Washington, DC.

Printed in Great Britain

ISBN 1-57409-161-1

Note: While all reasonable care has been taken in the
publication of this book, the publisher takes no
responsibility for the use of the methods or products
described in the book.

Contents

Preface   vii
Acknowledgements   viii
Terms and abbreviations   ix

Part 1
Chapter 1 • **Radio basics**   1

Frequencies and wavelengths   1
The radio spectrum   3
Modulation   4
Propagation of different frequencies   9

Chapter 2 • **VHF, HF and MF:**
Mainstays of marine communications 14

Licensing requirements:
   Radio operator qualifications and
   authorisation   14
   Ship radio licence   15
Marine VHF radio equipment; channels,
   effective range and the 'capture' effect   16
Marine MF and HF radio equipment   19

Chapter 3 • **GMDSS – the Global**
Maritime Distress and Safety System 22

Distress and safety communications
   before GMDSS   22
Digital Selective Calling (DSC)   24
Inmarsat satellite communications   30
Navtex   34

Emergency Position Indicating Radio
   Beacons (EPIRBs)   37
Search and Rescue Radar Transponders
   (SARTs)   39
Handheld VHF sets   40
Narrow Band Direct Printing (NBDP)
   telex   41
GMDSS: Strengths and weaknesses   41

Chapter 4 • **Amateur radio**   44

Amateur radio resources: nets,
   slow scan television, phone
   patches, e-mail   44
Amateur radio in an emergency   48
Amateur radio without a licence   49
Obtaining a licence   50
Learning Morse   51
Obtaining a licence outside your
   home country   51
Reciprocal licences   52

Chapter 5 • **Communications**
alternatives   54

Citizen Band (CB) radio   55
Family Radio Service   56
Cellular phones   56
Mobile satellite communications:
   Globalstar, Iridium, Inmarsat Mini-M,
   Inmarsat Fleet F77 and F55   59

Chapter 6 • **Equipment installation –**
demands made on the boat   66

Finding the power   66
Power for permanently installed
    equipment   69
Finding the energy   71
Radio interference   75
Protection against lightning   82
HF transceiver installation   82

Chapter 7 • **Marine antennas**   85

Basic ideas   85
Practical MF/HF antennas   88
Practical VHF antennas   98

Chapter 8 • **Computer modes**   101

Decoding data transmissions   101
Software decoders: Weatherfax,
    Polar orbiting satellite images,
    Slow scan television, Navtex,
    TOR (Telex On Radio) codes   104
Hardware data controllers and software   112

Chapter 9 • **E-mail and the internet**   116

HF e-mail services   117
FTPmail – web access by e-mail   121
YOTREPS passage reports   123
Full internet access   126

Part 2
1 • **Procedures, protocols**
and codes   127

Non-GMDSS Distress, Urgency and Safety   127
Requesting assistance   128
Simple form of Salvage Agreement   129

Reporting marine weather   130
The standard phonetic alphabet and
    numerals   132
Morse code   133
Extracts from the international Q code   134
Telex codes and abbreviations   137
The RST code   138
Maritime Mobile Service Identifiers (MMSI)   138

2 • **Frequency allocations**   142

Marine MF/HF – SSB channels and
    frequencies   142
SSB Simplex frequencies for ship to
    ship contacts   146
Marine VHF – channels and frequencies   147
Navtex stations and times of operation   150
Inmarsat-C SafetyNET™ broadcast times   160
MF, HF and VHF amateur frequencies   160
Amateur nets   161
International short wave broadcasts   161
USA Family Radio channels and
    frequencies   163

3 • **Technical data**   164

Radio transmission modes   164
Radio time signals and solar data   164
Battery data   165
Characteristics of common types of
    coax cable   166
The decibel (dB) scale   166

4 • **Further information**   168

Book list   168
Internet resources   169

Index   171

Preface

The past few years have seen more changes to marine communications than in any other period since the first use of radio at the beginning of the last century. From a time when it was common for even circumnavigators to carry no more than a basic VHF radio, we have moved to a time where far greater reliance is placed upon electronic technology. The introduction of the Global Marine Distress and Safety System (GMDSS) has changed not only the way in which distress signals are sent, but has had far reaching consequences for all marine communications.

When safety of life is not a factor, in addition to the GMDSS there are several other established and emerging technologies that can also be effectively used at sea. They provide access to a wealth of resources from weather charts, navigational updates, safety information, pilotage details, satellite images, business information, contacts with friends and family and general entertainment. Some services work only in certain areas, some require training or specialist installation, and equipment and running costs vary enormously. Some rely heavily upon satellites and the backing of multinational companies, but the, once thought to be futureless, HF radio has also seen a resurgence of interest now that new technologies have given it the ability to provide low cost e-mail.

About this book

Many books have been written as training manuals for marine radio operators. They give detailed coverage of basic radio operation and the procedures used in distress, urgency and safety messages but, as important as these topics are, this book has a much wider emphasis. Taking the subject a stage further, it introduces a broad range of communications services and equipment; compares one system with another and explains their benefits and shortcomings. Basic principles and theory are covered only to the extent that they are necessary for practical operation or to provide the understanding necessary to make temporary emergency repairs.

In Part 2, the reference information has been selected for the same reasons and includes items unlikely to be found in any other single source. In a book of this type it is impossible to give detailed user instructions on every system covered, so Part 2 also includes web links to suppliers and sources of further information.

Who this book is for

Even day sailors often dream of sailing away from their home shores and many actually achieve the ambition. This book is not just for long distance cruisers but for anyone looking for a broad overview of the current communications technologies that can be used aboard small craft. Included are skippers or operators of boats of all sizes, from ocean rowers through to the 300 gross registered tonnage lower SOLAS limit. In short, anyone wanting to know what options are available for establishing voice, e-mail and internet communications from a remote location at sea or on land.

Acknowledgements

In writing this book, many people have provided me with much help and encouragement. First, thanks go to my wife Di, for preparing the artwork, checking the text and continued support while I was writing it. Thanks are also due to Steve Williams for his professional perspective and to the American Amateur Radio Relay League for permission to include their Newsletter account of the Venezuelan pirate attack and subsequent rescue.

No book on small boat communications can be complete without acknowledging the contribution made by the amateur community. I am grateful for the continued help and guidance I have received from radio amateurs around the world and in particular those stalwart controllers of the UK maritime and Pacific Seafarer's nets. Others are sadly too numerous to mention. They come from many different countries, some ashore, some afloat, many I may never meet but without their friendship and support I would never have got started.

Mike Harris

Terms and abbreviations

Abbreviation	Meaning
AC	Alternating Current
ADSL	Asymmetrical Digital Subscriber Line
AF	Audio Frequency
AFSK	Audio Frequency Shift Keying
AMTOR/SITOR	Amateur and commercial implementations of telex on Radio (TOR see below)
AMVER	Automated Mutual-Assistance VEssel Rescue system
APT	Automatic Picture Transmission
ARPA	Automated Radar Plotting Aid
ARQ	Automatic Repeat Request
Baud	A unit of transmission speed and is the number of data line state changes per second
Bit	A single unit of binary data (ie 0 or 1)
BPS	Bits per second
Byte	The collection of bits that make up a binary word
C Band	4 to 8GHz portion of the electromagnetic spectrum
CEPT	European Conference of Postal Telecommunications Administrations
CES	Coast Earth Station
CMBO	WinLink 2000 Central Server
COLREGS	Convention on the International Regulations for Preventing Collisions at Sea (1972)
COSPAS	Russian acronym for space system for search of vessels in distress
CRC	Cyclic Redundancy Check
CRT	Cathode Ray Tube
CTCSS	Continuous Tone Coded Squelch System
DC	Direct Current
DCS	Digitally Coded Squelch
DGPS	Differential GPS
DSC	Digital Selective Calling

DSP	Digital Signal Processor
DTI	Department of Trade and Industry (UK)
EC	European Community
EGC	Enhanced Group Calling
EMC	Electro Magnetic Compatibility
EPIRB	Emergency Position Indicating Radio Beacon
FCC	Federal Communications Commission (US)
FEC	Forward Error Correction
FRS	Family Radio Service (US)
FSK	Frequency Shift Keying
GEOs	Geostationary satellite (approximately 36000km)
GMDSS	Global Maritime Distress and Safety System
GMT	Greenwich Mean Time (see Z below
GPS	Global Positioning System
GPRS	General Packet Radio Service
GSM	Global System for Mobile Communications
HF	High Frequency (3MHz to 30MHz) (ie short wave)
HRU	Hydrostatic Release Unit
IMO	International Maritime Organisation
Inmarsat	International Maritime Satellite Organisation
ISDN	Integrated Service Digital
ISP	Internet Service Provider
ITA	International Telegraph Alphabet
ITU	International Telecommunications Union
Ka Band	18 to 31GHz portion of the electromagnetic spectrum
Ku Band	10.9 to 17GHz portion of the electromagnetic spectrum
L Band	0.5 to 2GHz portion of the electromagnetic spectrum
LEOs	Low Earth Orbiting satellite (approximately 1500km)
LES	Land Earth Station
LESO	Land Earth Station Operator
LF	Low Frequency (30kHz to 300kHz)
LSB	Lower Side Band
LUT	Local User Terminal
LW	Long Wave (ie low frequency see LF)
MARS	Maritime mobile Access Retrieval System
MEOs	Medium Earth Orbiting satellite (approximately 10,000 to 20,000km)
MF	Medium Frequency (300kHz to 3MHz)
MOB	Man (applies to either gender) Overboard

Mobile (noun)	Cellular phone
MRCC	Maritime Rescue Coordination Centre
MSI	Maritime Safety Information
MW	Medium Wave (ie Medium Frequency see MF)
Navtex	Navigational information transmitted as FEC SITOR
NBDP	Narrow Band Direct Printing (ie radio telex)
NCS	Network Coordinating Station (satellite control station)
NIST	National Institute of Standards and Technology (US)
NOAA	National Oceanographic and Atmospheric Administration
NWS	National Weather Service (US)
PDA	Personal Digital Assistant; pocket-sized computer used to store contact details, schedules, and handle e-mails etc
PMBO	WinLink 2000 Participating Network Station
POB	People On Board (number of)
PSK	Phase Shift Keying
RAL	Radio Amateur Licensing Unit
RCC	Rescue Coordination Centre
RDF	Radio Direction Finding
RF	Radio Frequency
RMS	Root Mean Square
RT	Radio Telephone
RYA	Royal Yachting Association
S Band	2 to 4GHz portion of the electromagnetic spectrum
SARSAT	Search and Rescue Satellite
SART	Search And Rescue radar Transponder
SES	Ship Earth Station
SIM	Subscriber Identification Module (for mobile phones)
SITOR	Simplex Telex On Radio
SOLAS	Safety Of Life At Sea convention
SSTV	Slow Scan Television
SW	Short Wave (ie High Frequency)
SWR	Standing Wave Ration
TNC	Terminal Node Controller
TOR	Telex on Radio
TVI	Television Interference
UHF	Ultra High Frequency (300MHz to 30GHz)
UMTS	Universal Mobile Telecommunications System
URL	Uniform Resource Locator

USB	Upper Side Band, in the context of RF modulation or Universal Serial Bus, when referring to computer interfacing
UTC	Coordinated Universal Time (see Z below)
VHF	Very High Frequency (30MHz to 300MHz)
VLF	Very Low Frequency (3KHz to 30KHz)
WARC	World Administrative Radio Conference
WT	Wireless Telegraphy
X band	9.2 to 9.5GHz portion of the electromagnetic spectrum
Z	Zulu time which, for the purpose of this book, is synonymous with GMT or UTC

PART ONE
Chapter 1 • Radio basics

Visual and sound signals apart, radio is an integral part of virtually all small boat communications. As wires and fibre optic cables are to the shore based telephone networks, so, at sea, radio is the conduit through which we send messages and signals. Just as we use land phone lines to pass voice messages, fax or internet data, so too can we use marine radio in a similar way to make phone calls, pass e-mails and handle weatherfax and navigational data. Further than that, we can use radio in crew overboard alarms, position locators and as an intrinsic part of virtually all forms of electronic navigation, including GPS.

No understanding of marine communications systems could be complete without looking at the principles on which it works, and sometimes more importantly, those that might stop it from working. The following text does not pretend to provide a rigorous 'first principles' scientific explanation; for this, you will need to refer to standard texts on electromagnetic theory. However, it's hoped that there is just enough here for you to gain a handle on some fundamental principles which are not always intuitive.

Frequencies and wavelengths

Look through any radio programme guide and the chances are that somewhere you'll find a table listing the names of stations and their working 'frequencies' and possibly a mention of 'wavelengths' or 'wave bands'. Such terms are part of the lingua franca of radio and are used freely and often, but what do they mean and what are radio waves?

Unfortunately, none of our five senses equips us with the ability to detect radio waves, so instead it's helpful to construct a mental model comparing them with other physical effects that we can actually hear, see and feel. A good analogy can be a great help, although to avoid deeper confusion it should never be taken too literally.

As a starting point, let's consider the waves that appear on the surface of a smooth pond when you throw in a stone. Evenly spaced waves spread out across the surface and reach all parts. In this case, waves are formed between the surface of the water and the air. Although invisible, sound waves are another familiar example. Drop a book at one end of a room and the sound is heard at the other. These waves are transmitted through the air as tiny but rapid changes in pressure. Pluck a violin string and you can see it vibrating as it sets up pressure waves in the air around it, but these waves cannot pass through a vacuum and radio waves can, so in this case, what exactly is it that's waving?

Radio waves are often described as electromagnetic waves, and herein lies the clue. In fact, they consist of two waves, one *electrical* and one *magnetic* and, like the changes in pressure associated with a sound wave, they consist of changes in electrical and magnetic field strengths. Fig 1.1 shows a diagram of the pair of waves that are set at right angles to each other but move in the same direction. Unlike the water surface waves, they have nothing comparable to the air/water boundary but, instead, strengths of the electric and magnetic components diminish as distance from the central axis is increased.

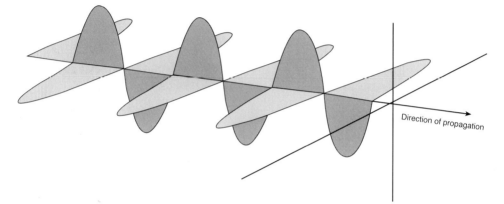

Fig 1.1 Electric and magnetic components of a 3-dimensional radio wave are at right angles to each other.

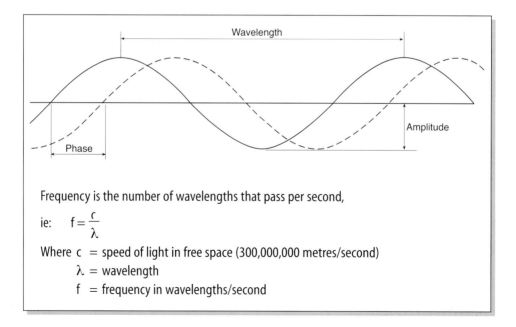

Frequency is the number of wavelengths that pass per second,

ie: $f = \dfrac{c}{\lambda}$

Where c = speed of light in free space (300,000,000 metres/second)
       λ = wavelength
       f = frequency in wavelengths/second

Units

1 wavelength/second = 1 hertz (Hz)

1kHz = 1,000 Hz

1MHz = 1,000,000 Hz

1GHz = 1,000,000,000 Hz

Radio waves can be described in terms of wavelength or frequency, with the relationship as follows:

Frequency (in MHz) = 300/wavelength (in metres)

Wavelength (MHz) = 300/frequency (in MHz)

Phase is a term used to compare the relationship with another associated wave. In the above example the dotted wave has the same frequency and amplitude and occupies the same position in space though it is slightly displaced from the solid wave. The displacement is usually measured as an angle where one whole wavelength = 360°.

Fig 1.2 Wave terminology.

The radio spectrum

In addition to radio waves, the electro-magnetic spectrum includes a vast range of different types of radiation of which visible light, with frequencies between 10^{14} and 10^{15}, is but a small part. Such huge numbers are hard to visualise but are like one oscillation per second for every grain of sand on all the beaches in Mexico. Convert this to wave-lengths and we get values of around 10^{-6} metres (ie 1μm or one millionth of a metre).

Progressing down through the frequency scale, immediately below visible light is the infrared spectrum, which we can feel as heat. Lower still and we reach the microwave region of the radio spectrum, with applications in radar, satellite communications and GPS. Still lower are the 'Very High Frequencies' (VHF) familiar to coastal sailors, and below these the 'High Frequencies' (HF) that, from the time of the *Titanic* to the present day, are still the mainstay of long distance marine communications.

Fig 1.3 gives a general overall plan of the relationship between bands within the spectrum, but just as you would be unable to see individual towns and streets on a map of the world, so the diagram is unable to show the great complexity with which regulatory authorities have subdivided each section. Notice how, particularly within the HF range, smaller bands of frequencies are allocated for marine use and that these are interleaved with similar bands for radio amateurs. Even within each of these sections there are often further subdivisions, with spot frequencies or channels designated for specific uses. Take, for example, the Marine VHF section that extends

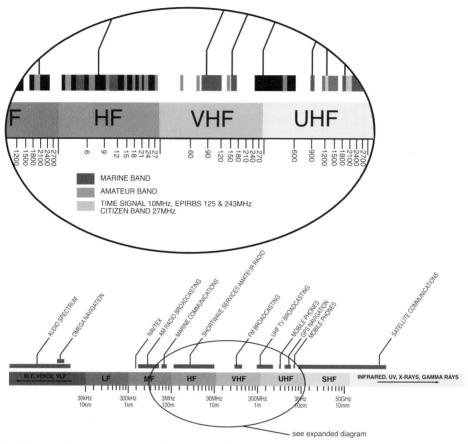

Fig 1.3 The radio spectrum from low frequencies to light.

between 150MHz and 170MHz and where particular channels are used exclusively for calling or communicating between ships or port authorities. Page 147 in Part 2 gives the finer details.

Not shown in Fig 1.3 are sections allocated for use by aircraft, police, emergency services, military, government agencies, taxis, entertainment and news broadcasters, model aircraft enthusiasts, radio astronomers and for a host of other services. Each contend vigorously for their share of bandwidth, which is determined periodically by the World Administrative Radio Conference (WARC).

Modulation

When received by a radio tuned a few kHz away, the pure single frequency shown in Fig 1.1, or carrier in Fig 1.4, sounds as a pure audio tone (of frequency equal to the difference between the carrier frequency and radio's tuned frequency.) This is fine as far as it goes, though virtually useless for communications as it conveys no useful information other than to say that the transmitter is turned on. What is needed is a method of mixing the carrier with a second signal that actually carries useful information. The process is known as *modulation*

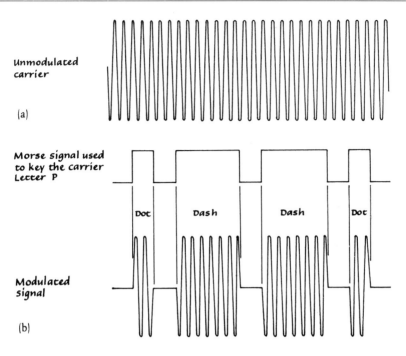

Fig 1.4 Modulating or 'keying' a carrier with a Morse letter P.

and in its most basic form this may consist of a simple scheme for turning the carrier on or off at timed intervals, as in Fig 1.4. Such a method is used to transmit Morse code, the system of short and long (ie 'dot' and 'dash') tones that has been used since the very earliest days of radio and which survives today as sound signals in the International Regulations for the Prevention of Collisions at Sea (COLREGS).

Audio speech frequencies are generally much lower than radio frequencies, but by using a microphone to convert them to an electrical signal, these too can be used to modulate a radio signal. There are a number of ways in which this can be achieved.

Amplitude modulation – AM

This is the oldest method of speech modulation, shown diagrammatically in Fig 1.5.

A characteristic of amplitude modulation is that the signal also occupies a set of frequencies a little above and below that of the carrier signal. This is known as *bandwidth* (see Table 1.1) and is inevitable with any method of modulation, though, in the case of AM, is particularly wide. Seventy years ago

Transmission type	Bandwidth
Morse	>100Hz
Radio Telex, eg Navtex	100Hz
Weatherfax	2kHz
SSB communications	3kHz
AM communications	6kHz
Music	15kHz
Computer data	1MHz
Colour television (625 line)	5.5MHz

Table 1.1 Typical bandwidths of various types of radio signals.

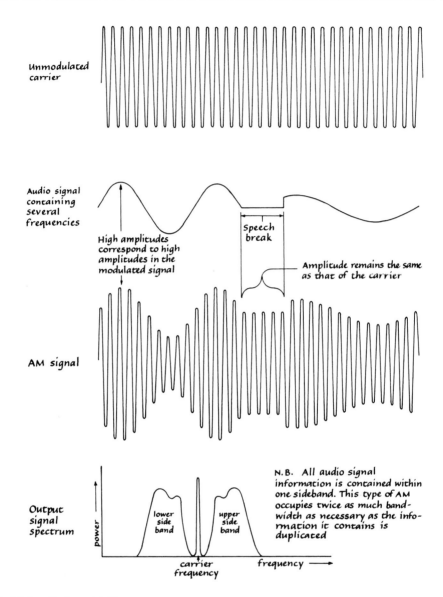

Fig 1.5 Amplitude modulation.

this was not so important, but now with so many users competing for a relatively limited amount of spectrum it's an important factor.

Although the normal human audio range is between 20Hz and 16kHz, perfectly good conversations can be held by using only those frequencies that fall within the range 2.4kHz to 3kHz. This does not give what might be called hi-fi reproduction, and would be unsuitable for music, but by using this restricted range the bandwidth of the modulated signal can be reduced, and more separate conversations can be packed into a given section of radio spectrum. This is the usual practice for marine communications channels, though not for commercial radio broadcasts.

Single side band – SSB

Today, amplitude modulation is almost never used for marine communications and has been replaced by single side band. This type of modulation has the advantage of a narrower bandwidth and also makes more effective use of transmitter power. The disadvantage is that SSB transmitters are rather more complex than those for AM, but with current micro-electronic technology this is no longer an important factor.

In essence, most SSB transmitters work by producing a conventional AM signal, then filtering out part or all of the carrier wave

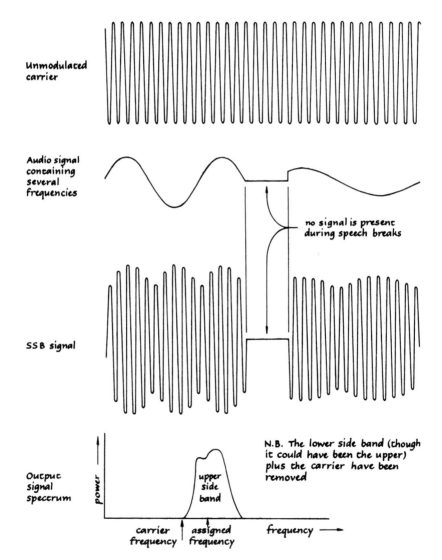

Fig 1.6 Single side band modulation.

along with all frequencies to one side of it. With upper side band SSB, only frequencies above the carrier are transmitted and with lower side band SSB, only the lower frequencies are transmitted.

Frequency modulation – FM

With frequency modulation, the amplitude of the transmitted signal does not change but its frequency is varied by the audio modulating signal. Fig 1.7 shows how.

When compared with AM or SSB, an advantage of FM is that signals are usually received with lower background noise levels.

Set against this is the disadvantage that FM requires a wider bandwidth. For this reason it is generally only used on VHF and higher frequencies, where more space is available. It is the method used for marine VHF, for high quality local radio broadcasts and in some countries for CB radio.

Before leaving this section, be aware of the system used to designate different types of modulation that's given in Part 2 on page 164. This is often used by manufacturers in sales literature and equipment manuals and can be confusing if you are unaware of the convention.

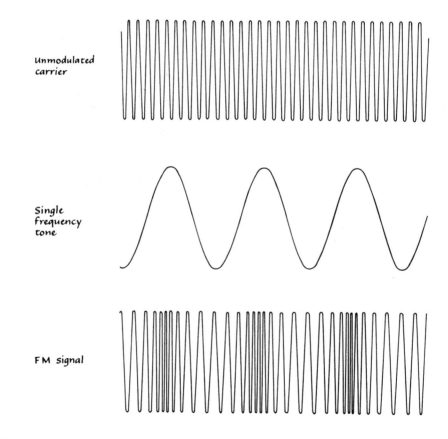

Unmodulated carrier

Single frequency tone

FM signal

Fig 1.7 Frequency modulation.

Propagation of different frequencies

Different parts of the radio spectrum have vastly different properties. Consider, for example, the difference between light that can be blocked by a sheet of card and medical X-rays that pass easily through soft tissue but not bone.

Radio signals can also pass through most non-metallic structures, and like light, those in the VHF band and above travel in straight lines. For this reason, the range achievable with marine VHF is approximately line of sight, ie we can communicate with any other station that is in direct sight of our vessel but not those that are beyond our horizon and masked by the Earth's curvature. If this were true for the entire radio spectrum, long range communications would be impossible, so how is it that in practice we are able to listen to short wave broadcast stations from the other side of the world?

The answer lies in the *ionosphere*, a part of the upper atmosphere that consists of a series of layers of ionised gases. These surround the earth and have the property of being able to bend certain radio frequencies (between 5 and 50MHz), causing them to be returned to earth. In this way they can be received at very great distances from the transmitter, well beyond the optical line of sight. By repeated reflection between Earth and the ionosphere, such signals may even be received on opposite parts of the globe.

Within the upper atmosphere, ions are formed when gas molecules lose electrons. The energy for the process comes from collisions with X, ultraviolet or other sun radiation, but the transition is reversible and the freed electrons are able to combine with ions to reform gas molecules. At any particular time, the proportions of molecules in an ionised state (the degree of ionisation) will depend upon the prevailing level of radiation and, as a result, more ionisation will occur over those parts of the earth that are in daylight. In this way, radio propagation tends to follow a daily pattern so that you may notice better radio reception from stations that lie towards the direction of the sun, rather than from those in darkness.

In addition to these diurnal changes there are also seasonal changes, as well as an important 11-year cycle following the sunspot activity. Sunspots usually accompany high levels of solar radiation, which in turn lead to increased ion production and, because higher levels of ionisation are required to refract the higher frequencies, these are times when some frequencies, particularly between 20Mhz to 30MHz, can be used to cover large distances; an effect that sometimes surprises Citizen Band (CB) radio enthusiasts, who suddenly find

Marine antenna height (metres)	Shore station antenna height (metres)				
	1.5	3	7.5	30	75
1.5	5	7	9	15	23
3	9	10	11	18	25
10	10	12	13	20	25
20	12	14	15	21	30

Table 1.2 Approximate VHF range achievable (in miles) at differing antenna heights above sea level.

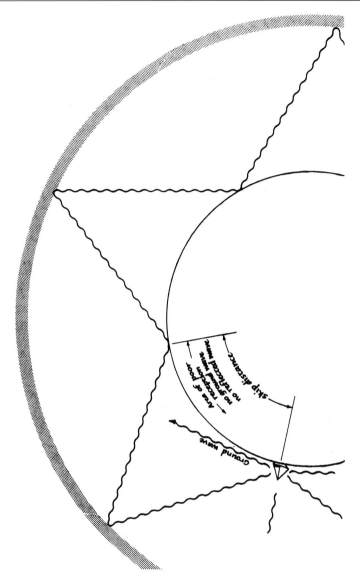

Fig 1.8 Refraction of high frequency radio waves and the skip zone.

that they are able to talk with stations on other continents using radios that are usually only able to reach the next village or city.

A measure of solar activity that is related to the sunspot numbers is given by the solar flux, which usually has values of between 50 and 300. Current solar flux values are transmitted periodically by radio stations

WWV and WWVH and are available from several internet sites (see page 169).

Ionospheric layering

The layering shown in Fig 1.9 is typical of that found during the daytime. At night, when the sun's radiations are absent, the D and E layers

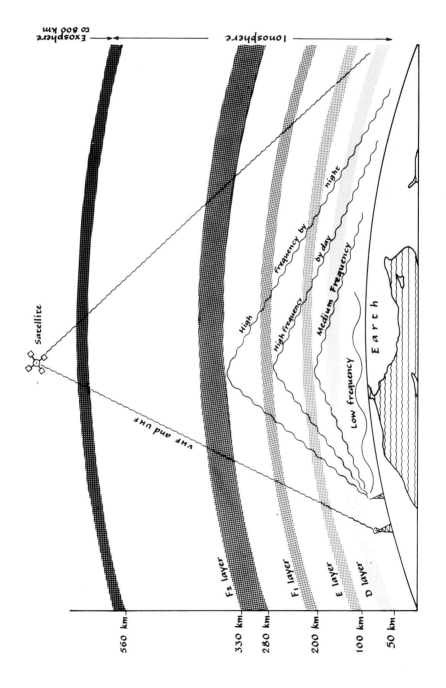

Fig 1.9 Daytime arrangement of ionised layers within the ionosphere.

tend to disappear whereas the F1 and F2 layers merge and form a single F layer which is mainly responsible for long distance night propagation. Ion densities and heights of all layers can change depending upon solar conditions but each has its own characteristic effect upon radio propagation.

F, F1 and F2 layers

During the day the highest layer is the F2 which also has the highest ion density and so is capable of returning frequencies around 22MHz near to the top end of the HF range. This is useful in covering distances of 2500 miles (4022km) or more.

F1 layer

When the F1 is not combined with the F2, it is less highly ionised and is capable of returning frequencies of the mid HF and is used for distances of around 2000 miles (3218km).

E layer

This has an even lower ion density but is effective in returning lower frequency signals. These are useful in covering distances of a few hundred to 1500 miles (2413km).

D layer

This has the lowest ion density and tends to absorb rather than refract radio signals. Higher ion densities in this layer tend to produce fading on HF bands.

Deep fading

Sometimes, following solar flares, the sun produces abnormal amounts of ultra-violet and X radiation which lead to greatly increased levels of ionisation in the lower D layers. This has the effect of absorbing rather than reflecting radio waves, and during these times HF radio communications may be totally lost. For a few minutes, or maybe hours, it is possible to tune across the bands and hear nothing other than sounds like distant bacon frying. The effect is known as a `Sudden Ionospheric Disturbance' (SID) or `Dellinger' fade-out. A few days after the SID another kind of intense fading, the `ionospheric storm', may follow. This is thought to be caused by the arrival of slower moving particles from the same flare.

Geomagnetic effects

Charged particles from the sun, and from solar flares in particular, are attracted by the earth's magnetic field and tend to concentrate in polar regions. A measure of these effects is the Boulder K index, which has values between 0 and 9. High values are associated with high absorption of signals crossing polar regions. As with solar flux, the Boulder K index is also broadcast by stations WWV and WWVH and available from the internet.

Finding out which frequencies are available

In summary, propagation of HF radio signals is affected by a number of factors including solar activity, ionospheric conditions, season and time of day, making it difficult to predict exactly which frequencies will give best reception for a particular route and time of day. There are few hard and fast rules and experience and intuition are useful but they take time to acquire.

Table 1.3 gives a rough starting point but in addition:

Frequency band (MHz)	Day time range (miles)	Night time range (miles)
1.5 to 3	Ground wave only	1000
3 to 6	Ground wave only	1500
6 to 10	600	2000
10 to 16	1800	Worldwide in the direction of the sun
16 to 23	3000	Worldwide in the direction of the sun until 20:00 local time
22 to 30	Maybe worldwide but depends on ionisation	Little sky wave reflection after sunset

Table 1.3 Typical ranges achievable by various frequencies in the HF band.

• *Listen to your radio*

Listening in to beacons and traffic lists will tell you which bands are open, and by listening regularly you will be able to build up your own picture of propagation changes.

• *If you can hear them, they will hear you*

There are many reasons why this rule should not work. Perhaps the station that you are listening to has a better antenna and/or is using more power than you, but used with care it can be a guide to choosing a working frequency.

• *Use your own propagation prediction software*

Written for Windows®, HF-Prop (shown in Fig 1.10) predicts optimum frequencies for a given route, date and value of solar flux and Boulder K index. Designed for use at sea, it can be run without an internet connection and is available as a free 30-day trial download before you buy.

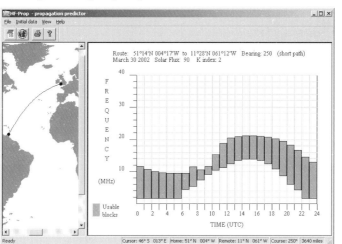

Fig 1.10 HF-Prop propagation predictor software showing fequencies for the route Bristol (UK) to Trinidad (www.pangolin.co.nz).

Chapter 2 • VHF, HF and MF: Mainstays of marine communications

Before looking at marine radio equipment in detail we begin this chapter with a review of the licensing and legal requirements needed to operate it. Each country administers its own national licensing scheme, with overall regulation carried out on an international basis in accordance with the Radio Regulations of the International Telecommunication Union (ITU). As a result, there are broad similarities between the licensing procedures of different countries and it's these similarities that we will concentrate on here. There are some differences in detail and before applying for a licence you are advised to contact your own national communications authority and obtain the latest and most up to date information.

Licensing requirements

The use of marine radio equipment is covered by three different types of certification: operator qualifications, vessel licences and the equipment itself, which must meet particular design criteria.

Radio operator qualifications and authorisation

Two types of marine radio operator qualifications/licences most likely to interest small boat users are:

1 VHF operator certificates (short range)
2 MF and HF operator certificates (long range)

The VHF certificate is a bare minimum basic requirement for coastal sailors whose voyages do not extend beyond the range of local coastal radio (ie GMDSS Sea Area 1 – see page 23). Obtaining the licence involves a short course of instruction in operating procedures, with particular emphasis on how to make and respond to distress, urgency and safety messages. Often this, and the final examination, can be completed within a day.

For those travelling further afield, the HF and MF certificate is required and can also include use of satellite communications. Here the course of instruction includes elements on:

• VHF, MF and HF communications
• DSC (Digital Selective Calling)
• Navtex
• Use of EPIRBs and SARTs
• Practical operation of Inmarsat-C
• Capabilities of various Inmarsat systems
• The role of Inmarsat within the GMDSS

The GMDSS (Global Maritime Distress and Safety System) and associated topics are covered in Chapter 3. Candidates are examined on:

- Radio regulations
- In-depth knowledge of Distress, Urgency and Safety procedures
- Practical handling of Distress, Urgency and Safety traffic
- Practical operation of equipment

Within the past few years, the introduction of the GMDSS has made big changes in radio operator licensing and those with qualifications issued under the earlier system are required to retrain and upgrade.

The ship radio licence

Ship radio licences are issued to vessels and their individual owners and are not transferable to other vessels or other owners. They are renewable annually and cover the use of:

- MF, HF, VHF equipment
- Digital Selective Calling (DSC) equipment associated with the Global Maritime Distress & Safety System (GMDSS)
- Satellite communications equipment (Ship Earth Stations)
- RADAR; Search and Rescue Radar Transponders (SARTs)
- Low powered, onboard maritime UHF communications equipment
- Onboard repeater stations
- 121.5/123.1MHz Aeronautical Search and Rescue equipment
- 121.5/243MHz and 406/121.5MHz Personal Locator Beacons (PLBs), 406MHz and 1.6GHz Emergency Position Indicating Radio Beacons (EPIRBs).

Set out in the licence are a number of conditions including:

a A list of permitted frequencies
b The maximum transmitter power that may be used
c The type of modulation
d Types of stations that can be contacted
e Types of messages that may be passed
f Only permits the station to be operated under the control of a holder of a certificate of competence and authority to operate

Callsigns

Callsigns are issued along with the first application for a ship licence and remain with the vessel indefinitely; even after a change of ownership. Their purpose is to identify stations accurately for the following reasons:

1 Many boats share the same name but callsigns are unique. Their use in an emergency is a concise and unambiguous way of confirming the correct identity of a vessel
2 For use in locating sources of interference
3 For correct billing of commercial services

Maritime Mobile Service Identifiers (MMSI)

Like the callsign, these are also used to identify the vessel but are for use with GMDSS equipment and are explained on page 25. They are also issued with the licence and need to be programmed into DSC equipment by a qualified technician.

Selcall Numbers

This is another identifier, also issued by the licensing authority, and is programmed into radio telex equipment. They enable it to respond automatically to calls addressed to it.

The Maritime Mobile Access and Retrieval System (MARS) database

The ITU requires licensing authorities to provide information about licensed vessels and the equipment they carry. This includes the above identifiers and the information is held in the ITU's MARS database and is made available to Port Authorities and search and rescue organisations throughout the world. (www.itu.int/cgi-bin/htsh/mars/mars_index.sh)

marine communications. It has no competitor and is used extensively for distress and safety traffic, intership messages, port operations and public correspondence throughout the world.

Marine VHF has been around for more than half a century and, while there have been revolutionary changes to the internal design, the basic controls remain much the same and include an on/off switch, volume control,

---

Radio equipment conformity requirements

For marine radio equipment manufacturers to sell their products, they must first ensure that they conform to a rigorous set of design criteria. These define parameters such as frequency range, method of changing frequency, power output, other control functions and many finer details.

Once again, the exact requirements can vary between countries and there are also differences between equipment intended for commercial vessels and for pleasure craft. The EU, for example, has a mandatory system that requires manufacturers to operate their own production and quality control processes. On the other hand, the US has a system of production test and inspection processes that often involves independent laboratories. The good news is that resolution of these differences is taking place, although there are other nations with conflicting standards so it may be some time before a marine radio bought in one country is acceptable aboard vessels of another.

VHF radios are an example of this. Those sold in the US generally include a number of weather information channels and UK radios include special marina frequencies, but neither of these uses is supported elsewhere.

Marine VHF radio equipment

For large numbers of small craft users, marine VHF will meet their entire communications needs. The equipment is compact, simple, reliable, fairly easy to install, gives good quality speech, and because propagation does not rely upon the vagaries of the ionosphere, there is relatively little background noise. Marine VHF is the workhorse of short-range

squelch (sensitivity) adjustment, low/high power switch and channel switch.

Channels

The part of the radio spectrum used for marine VHF occupies the section between 156MHz and 174MHz, but to make operating procedures easier this has been subdivided into numbered channels. These are given in

Fig. 2.1 The facia mounted ICS VHF3 transceiver (bottom unit) with its accompanying DSC3 digital selective calling unit (courtesy of ICS Electronics Ltd)

Part 2 page 147 and on looking down the list you will notice that some channels (eg 16) are both transmitted and received on the same frequency. These are known as *simplex* channels and in practice this means that a pair of people in conversation cannot both speak at the same time. Rather as one would speak to someone through a length of hose-pipe, you listen while the other person speaks and you end with the word *over* to indicate that it's now the listener's turn to speak and your turn to listen.

Other channels, such as those for public correspondence, are designated as *duplex* and are transmitted on one frequency and received on another. In principle, this makes it possible to hold a normal telephone-like conversation, where both people may speak at the same time. Having only one antenna, most small craft radios are not able to transmit and receive at the same time but mimic duplex operation by carrying out the transmit/receive frequency shift. This is described as *semi-duplex* operation.

In listening to, say, a coast radio station, using a duplex channel to talk to another vessel, you will hear only the coast station side of the conversation, since your radio would be configured with the same transmit and receive frequencies. However, the coast station would have the complementary configuration, ie transmitting on your receive frequency and vice versa. In this way, it is impossible for two ship station radios to communicate with each other on coast radio station duplex channels.

Channel 16 (156.800MHz)

Channel 16 is designated as the international Distress, Urgency, Safety and Calling radio-telephony channel. Where it is necessary to call a station on Channel 16, other than in cases of distress, urgency or safety, both stations should switch to an alternative working channel as soon as possible. In the case of calls between ship stations, this should be one of the intership channels (eg 6, 8, 72, or 77).

All calls should be kept as brief as possible and, other than for distress, urgency or safety traffic, should be of less than one minute duration.

Channel 70 (156.525MHz)

Since the introduction of GMDSS, this is now the primary channel for distress, urgency and safety alerting using DSC. It can also be used to initiate routine calls using DSC but must not be used for voice communications. Where practicable, vessels equipped with DSC should also keep a listening watch on Channel 16 at least until 1 February 2005 or until the full transition to DSC is complete in their area. It is strongly recommended that all radios without DSC be replaced by this time.

Channel 13 (156.650MHz)

This channel is used for bridge to bridge voice communications under GMDSS. It is normally monitored by commercial vessels if a danger of collision exists. It is one of the few that under GMDSS can be used without a preceding DSC alert on Channel 70.

Channel 6 (156.300MHz)

Under GMDSS this is used for communications between ships and aircraft for co-ordinating search and rescue operations.

Effective range

As mentioned in the last chapter, VHF range is essentially line of sight. This may not seem a great deal but the restriction can be a distinct advantage. These days, when there are so many users making demands on the VHF system, it does allow more stations to make use of the same frequencies without interfering with each other. In this way, a great many more people are able to use the system than if the same services were carried out on, say, HF with world coverage.

However, responsible use of VHF still requires consideration for the needs of others and once you have established contact with another station, it is good practice to reduce transmitter power to the minimum required to maintain the conversation. Although you may not hear other stations, it is quite possible that there are others using the same frequency and by reducing power you reduce the possibility of causing interference to others, and also use a little less of your own battery power.

The 'Capture' effect

When using VHF, bear in mind that signals from a strong station will mask those from weaker stations. So if your signals are strong and you are in contact with another station with a similar signal strength, it is likely that neither of you will be able to hear a third, weaker station that may be trying to break in on your conversation.

Marine MF and HF radio equipment

Marine VHF is fine when you are within 30 or 40 miles of a coastal radio station, but at greater distances high and medium frequencies provide the simplest means of keeping in touch. If VHF radio is the workhorse for short range contacts, then for long range communications the same is certainly true for MF and particularly HF radios. A modern MF/HF transceiver is a most versatile piece of equipment and has many benefits by which it can earn its keep. For example:

- Long range contacts with coast stations
- Personal contacts with other boats beyond VHF range
- Can be used to call for assistance in an emergency or for advice for less severe difficulties
- HF e-mail and file transfer services (see Chapter 9)
- Reception of weather forecasts
- Weatherfax reception
- Reception of news and entertainment broadcasts
- Once you have the licence and the equipment, use of MF/HF is free

A disadvantage of MF/HF is that it is very much affected by ionospheric conditions and on any particular occasion some frequency bands will be more effective than others (See page 13, Chapter 1). Compared to VHF and satellite communications, background noise is likely to be greater and signals may sometimes fade or gain in strength.

Channels

Like Marine VHF, the MF and HF bands are also subdivided into channels (see Part 2, page 142) and are similarly allocated to specific purposes, such as distress, safety and calling, intership use, telephone connections and telex.

Installation

Installation of an MF/HF transceiver is a more complex process than installing a VHF transceiver. Critical points are:

- Provision of a suitable power supply
- Provision of an antenna tuner
- RF grounding

These aspects are covered in Chapters 6 and 7.

Fig 2.2 Barrett 980 HF marine transceiver (courtesy of Barrett Communications).

Differences between marine and amateur band transceivers

MF/HF transceivers sold for marine communications have much in common with those sold for use by radio amateurs or land mobile stations. All are built essentially as general purpose SSB transceivers, have a similar technical specification and usually include a good quality receiver that covers the entire range between 300kHz and 30MHz. So what exactly are the differences?

The main difference is in design philosophy, with the underlying idea that since marine radios may be used to obtain help in an emergency, their operation should be kept as simple as possible so that any member of the crew may use them effectively. With this in mind, marine radios have few operator controls. Memory channels are stored with operating frequencies so switching frequency is simply a matter of pushing a button to select another channel. These design characteristics form a part of the conformity requirements for marine radios and without them a manufacturer would be unable to market its products for this purpose.

On an amateur transceiver, instead of fixed channels, the operating frequency is usually continuously variable and set via a large knob on the front panel. There is no shortage of other controls too, and these can include noise reduction filters, a speech compressor, separate RF and AF gain controls, an output power control (useful for conserving battery power) and sometimes a multitude of other functions.

Fig 1.3 shows how maritime frequencies are interleaved with those allocated for amateur use. In a new marine band transceiver as supplied by the factory, internal programming allows it to transmit only on marine band frequencies. Similarly, a factory-fresh amateur band radio is set to transmit only on the amateur bands. However, the internal adjustment needed to enable one type of radio to transmit on the frequencies of the other is often quite simple, though it may not be well documented.

Some owners, perhaps not having the space or funds to install both types, may be tempted to install one and adapt it to cover the frequencies of the other. In some countries there are legal restrictions that prohibit the use of amateur transceivers on marine bands and carry extraordinarily stiff penalties. It is the licensee's responsibility to ensure that all maritime radio covered by the vessel's licence does in fact meet the relevant requirements.

As a piece of equipment that could be used to save lives, the operating complexity of amateur gear is a factor to be considered. If you have unskilled crew members, circumstances could occur where, in an emergency, they are left as the only ones able to call for assistance. It would be a tragedy if some trivial but wrong adjustment setting prevented their call from being heard.

For this reason, a marine transceiver is often the radio of choice but channelised frequency selection is often difficult to use on amateur bands, where one is regularly required to make small frequency adjustments. As is explained in Chapter 4, only licensed amateurs are permitted to transmit on amateur frequencies. Emergency use is the exception to this rule, which could be a good reason to ensure that they are made available if needed.

Why bother with MF/HF if you have a satellite system?

It is sometimes argued in sales literature that if one has a GMDSS satellite communication system and a simple receiver for picking up weather information, an MF/HF transceiver is unnecessary. This ignores the fact that MF/HF has a long-established community of users that one would be unable to contact. As an example, in the North Atlantic, Caribbean and eastern Pacific, *Southbound II*'s free weather routing service (see page 170) has been used by thousands of cruising boats over many years. Herb Hilgenburg, who operates the station and who tailors forecasts to the special needs of individual callers, can give little help to those only able to listen. Consider too, that large numbers of cruising boats already carry MF/HF transceivers but few use satellite gear. If you're considering a passage to a foreign port and need to check out details of official formalities or mooring details, the best advice often comes from other boats that have just experienced them. HF radio nets are the way that most people meet and exchange such details. And because use of the airwaves is free they attract many participants. In satellite terms, the equivalent would be a conference call but, even if more boats carried the equipment, service charges would be a strong deterrent.

Finally, if you are considering buying an MF/HF receiver, look closely at the specification and compare it to those provided as part of a transceiver. The receiver included with most transceivers is usually of a very high communications quality, far in excess of most lower priced broadcast receivers. Because more transceivers are sold, their cost is often not greatly different from that of stand alone receivers of similar quality.

Chapter 3 • GMDSS – the Global Maritime Distress and Safety System

Introduced by the International Maritime Organisation (IMO), the GMDSS is the most significant development in marine communications for a number of decades. From 1 February 1999 it became compulsory for all vessels subject to the international Safety of Life At Sea (SOLAS) convention Chapter IV. This generally includes all passenger vessels and all cargo ships of over 300 gross registered tons on international voyages. In some flag states, it is also a requirement for coastal voyages. Although most small craft fall outside of this category and are not compelled to adopt the system, in some regions failure to do so could isolate them from useful sources of weather and safety information and, should they need to summon help, could mean that there is no one listening for their call.

In this chapter, we take a broad overview of the GMDSS, its associated equipment and some of its difficulties and shortcomings. For details of operating procedures and protocols, readers are referred to the standard operator examination texts listed in *A Boater's Guide to VHF and GMDSS* by Sue Fletcher. Since the GMDSS is still a fairly new concept, it is still evolving and over the coming years considerable changes can be expected.

Distress and Safety Communications before GMDSS

From the sinking of the *Titanic* in 1912 up to the mid-1990s, fundamental long distance marine communications tools were the MF and HF transceivers. For short range use, VHF transceivers, introduced in the 1950s and 60s, quickly became very popular, and on many small craft today are the only radio carried. Inmarsat satellite services were also introduced but large antennas, heavy power consumption, and high running and equipment costs placed them beyond the means of most small craft operators.

Prior to 1999 ships and coastal radio stations were required to maintain listening watches on certain internationally designated voice channels (see Part 2 page 127) that are reserved solely for distress and making initial calls to other stations. Protocol for the use of these channels is well covered by the various marine radio operator courses so will not be explained in detail here, though procedures for distress, urgency and safety traffic are outlined in Part 2 page 127. This principle of using the same frequency for both purposes is an important one since, by encouraging all users to monitor these channels for routine calls, it increases the chances that a distress message would be heard by as many stations as possible. After the initial call with non-urgent traffic, stations are required to switch promptly to a working channel for the body of their conversation, and in this way the main distress/calling channel is kept clear.

For decades the system has worked well, and still continues to do so in many parts of the world. Unfortunately, it is less effective in regions where there are large numbers of vessels and where radio traffic is heavy. If a vessel needing to send a distress message is operating under difficulties, has a weak signal and has to wait for a quiet break in traffic before it can be sent, their chance of it being heard is poor. If there are other stations with more powerful signals wanting to make routine calls and who can't hear the distress station, they will see no reason not to go ahead, make the call and obliterate any hope of the distress signal being heard by anyone else.

There have been many examples of this type of event, particularly in busier European waters where, in addition to docking and departing ships, there are tug operations, passenger ferries, fishing vessels and, at holiday time, perhaps hundreds of small craft all within VHF range of each other. To alleviate the problem, in some areas coastal radio stations stopped responding to routine calls on Channel 16, accepting them only on their working channel. Marinas also adopted their own working channels, as did port control and Coastguard stations. But aboard ships at sea there were still more difficulties. Regulations required them to monitor not only Channel 16, but also the MF and HF distress frequencies. A constant background barrage of static and thunder crashes plus constant small boat chatter on Channel 16 often made it extremely difficult to filter out important information from the irrelevant, particularly

GMDSS coverage areas

To achieve worldwide coverage, GMDSS communications include VHF, MF and HF radio together with higher frequency Inmarsat satellite services. Based on the range limitations of each system and on the availability of local coastal radio stations, the world is divided into four sea areas.

Sea area	Boundaries	Equipment required
1	Area A1 lies within range of shore based VHF coast stations (approximately 20 to 30 nautical miles)	VHF
2	Area A2 excludes area A1 but lies within range of shore based MF coast stations (approximately 100 to 150 nautical miles)	VHF/MF
3	Area A3 excludes areas A1 and A2 but lies within the coverage of Inmarsat communications satellites (generally latitudes between 70° North and 70° South)	VHF/MF/HF or Inmarsat
4	Area A4 is all other sea areas (generally polar regions)	VHF/MF/HF

when operators are expected to carry out other duties at the same time. Overcoming these problems was a major objective of the GMDSS, which introduced a degree of automation to calling procedures through a process known as Digital Selective Calling.

Digital Selective Calling (DSC)

The only functional difference between a GMDSS radio and earlier types is an item known as the DSC controller. This could form an integral part of the radio or be a separate unit, as in Fig 2.1. Rather like a telephone pager, a call made on a DSC equipped radio is sent as a digitally encoded tone that only alerts the radio on the vessel for which the call is intended. Compare this to the older system of voice calling, where the message is heard through the loud speaker of every radio within range. But before looking at how the call is made in detail, we need to look at the data items that make up the initial digital call.

On making a DSC call, the digital signal sent by the calling station carries a packet of data, which includes the MMSI (Maritime Mobile Service Identity) described opposite that's stored in the radio along with other

Fig 3.1 The ICS TC2 communication system for GMDSS areas A1, A2 and A3 includes both VHF and MF/HF transceivers. The DSC control panel is the uppermost of the two main panel units. The small screen displays call details and, being touch sensitive, is used to program responses. The 'Distress' button is in the top left corner (courtesy of ICS Electronics Ltd).

information about the type of call that's being made. These details can include:

1 The MMSI of the station called.
2 The priority of the call, eg distress, urgency, safety or routine traffic.
3 If a distress call, an indication of the nature of the difficulty, eg sinking, fire, attack, MOB, collision, etc.
4 The vessel's position. This may have been entered by the operator or automatically if the DSC unit is interfaced to a GPS receiver.
5 A frequency and transmission mode on which to continue the communication.

Maritime Mobile Service Identity (MMSI)

Like a telephone number or radio callsign, every GMDSS vessel is issued by its radio licensing authority with a 9-digit MMSI. This is built in to all DSC and other GMDSS equipment, and except in special cases the equipment should not be transferred to another vessel. Once a radio is programmed with its MMSI, it cannot be changed by the user but only by a qualified technician.

Part of the MMSI is a 3-digit component known as the Maritime Service Identifier(MID) which indicates the issuing country. A list is given on page 148 and its placement within the MMSI is as follows:

Ship station identifiers

This begins with the MID and has the following form:

MIDXXXXXX

In this example, and in those that follow each X may be any digit between 0 and 9.

Group ship identifiers

These begin with zero and have the following form:

0MIDXXXXX

In this case the MID refers to the country that issued the MMSI and may not be the nationality of vessels within the group.

Coast station identifiers

These begin with two zeros and have the form:

00MIDXXXX

All US Coast Guard stations use the same MMSI (003669999) which, when used in a DSC call, will alert any that is within range.

Handheld VHF/DSC radios

In the UK a block of special MMSIs ending 900000 to 999999 has been reserved for these radios and can be moved from vessel to vessel.

Inmarsat equipment

The MMSI of a vessel equipped with Inmarsat-C will always have one trailing zero. Vessels equipped with Inmarsat-B and/or M will have three trailing zeros.

Beware: If you wish to install Inmarsat equipment but have an MMSI that does not follow this format, you will need to apply to your licensing authority for a replacement. You will also need to engage a qualified technician to re-program it into your DSC radio.

As with the old system of voice calling, the call is received and decoded by all DSC equipped radios within range but is ignored by all except the one (or ones) for which it is intended. On receipt, these radios respond by sounding an alarm signal and displaying the call details on a small screen. These include the channel to which the operator can switch to respond to the message, though on some sets the switching is automatic. So, while the calling part of the communication is a fully automated digital process, the continuing part of the conversation can be carried out on a conventional voice channel, exactly as in pre-GMDSS times.

Types of DSC call

The basic DSC concept after making an initial automated digital contact on a dedicated DSC channel is that stations switch to another channel to continue the conversation in voice or digital modes. Within this framework, there are four basic types of call that can be made. These are Distress, Urgency, Safety, and Routine calls, whose purposes exactly parallel their counterparts of the same name in the earlier system. Each is handled in a slightly different way, and the steps needed to initiate each are summarised in Table 3.1.

Distress Calls

These take priority over all other types of calls. Once a DSC Distress message is sent on VHF or MF, the radio will continue to retransmit the call at approximately four-minute intervals until an acknowledgement is received. As with Safety and Urgency calls, Distress calls are directed to all stations so all DSC enabled radios within range will respond by sounding an alarm and displaying the call details on their screens. Ideally, it will also be received by a shore based Rescue Co-ordination Centre (RCC), who with their extensive resources and training are best placed to manage the situation. Part of their response is to send a

Distress calls should only be sent on the authority of the master and when the vessel or people are in *grave and imminent danger* and in need of immediate assistance.

DSC distress acknowledgement, which on VHF and MF causes the distressed vessel's radio to stop sending its DSC MAYDAY. All further communications between the vessel and RCC are then continued on the corresponding radio telephone distress channel (Table 3.2).

Step	Distress	Urgency	Safety	Routine
1	Set the distress mode by pressing the distress button	Select Urgency on the control panel	Select Safety on the control panel	Select Routine on the control panel
2	Select the band on which the alert is to be transmitted (see Table 3.2)			
3	If time permits enter the boat's position at a given time and the nature of the distress	Address the call to 'all stations' or the MMSI of a required coast station, vessel or group of vessels	Address the call to the MMSI of the required coast station, vessel or group of vessels	Address the call to the MMSI of the required coast station or vessel
4	Key in the channel or in the case of MF & HF the frequency and mode # on which the follow-on message will be transmitted			
5	Transmit the DSC			

Mode refers to the transmission mode (see page 164 [designation of radio transmission modes]).

Table 3.1 Outline procedure for making Distress, Urgency, Safety or Routine DSC calls.

DSC frequency	Radio telephone frequency for Distress, Urgency or Safety traffic	Radio telex frequency for Distress, Urgency or Safety traffic
2187.5kHZ	2182.0kHz	2174.5
4207.5kHz	4125.0kHz	4177.5
6312.0kHz	6215.0kHz	6268.0
8414.5kHz	8291.0kHz	8376.5
12557.0kHz	12290.0kHz	12520.0
16805.5kHz	16420.0kHz	16695.0
VHF Channel 70	VHF Channel 16	

Table 3.2 DSC calling channels and their associated frequencies for Distress, Urgency and Safety traffic.

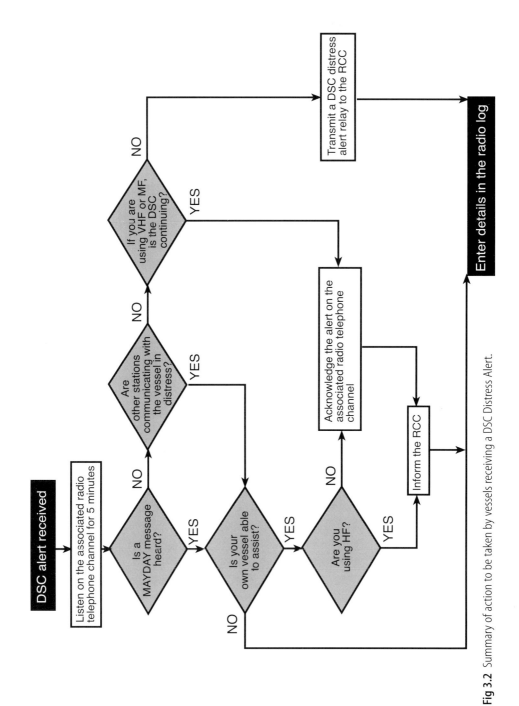

Fig 3.2 Summary of action to be taken by vessels receiving a DSC Distress Alert.

Responding to a Distress Alert

A DSC Distress Alert is signalled by an audio alarm, and a first priority for other ships is to discontinue any radio working that may interfere with communications between the RCC and the distressed vessel. Next, switch to the associated radio telephone channel and listen for five minutes to see if a MAYDAY voice message is sent and if the RCC or other stations have responded to the call. If they have, consider carefully your present position and that of the vessel in distress and decide if you are able to assist. If you are not, recording the details in your radio log is all that can be done. If you are, then contact the RCC to offer assistance, and if using VHF/MF then acknowledge the distress call on the associated radio telephone channel.

For vessels responding to a DSC Distress Alert, an important point to remember is **never** to send an immediate DSC Distress Acknowledgement (not to be confused with the radio telephone acknowledgement). On VHF/MF this causes the distressed vessel's radio to stop sending repeats of the message and could prevent the RCC from responding to the call.

So far, it has been assumed that after the initial DSC call all further communications will be carried out on a radio telephone (voice) channel. However, use of telex is an acceptable, albeit unusual, alternative with the distinct advantage that all parties will have a written copy of all correspondence. This can be especially useful if there are language difficulties or where advice given or received is particularly complex.

Types of DSC controllers

In this brief general discussion of DSC, it's not been possible to describe the full range of facilities and procedures. The situation is complicated by the way in which equipment from different manufacturers varies in

---

Cancellation of an inadvertent DSC Distress Alert

With DSC equipment it is certainly very easy to send a distress call and there is a correspondingly strong possibility that this could be done accidentally. To avoid a waste of search and rescue resources, it is essential to inform anyone that may have received it of the error. Steps to take are:

1 Prevent further repeat transmissions of the DSC Distress Alert. Switching off the transceiver is a sure way to do this, though a very few sets include the means to send a DSC self-cancellation.
2 Turn the transceiver back on and switch to the radio telephone channel associated with that on which the false alert was sent.
3 Transmit an All Stations Message giving the vessel's name, callsign and MMSI and say that the earlier Distress Alert was cancelled. Give also the time of the false alert. If the Distress Alert was transmitted on a number of frequencies, the cancellation message should be repeated on each of the associated frequencies.

operation and function. There are standards of course, but they are continually evolving and not always the same between countries and not always interpreted in quite the same way.

To illustrate the point, DSC controllers have been built to at least eight different classes or design specifications. Here are just a few:

Class A	Fulfils all IMO GMDSS requirements for MF and HF on SOLAS vessels.
Class B	Fulfils minimum IMO GMDSS requirements for MF and VHF.
Class C	A simplified class that has been found to be defective and dangerous and has been withdrawn.
Class D	Fulfils minimum requirements for VHF and follows European recommendations. At the time of writing, this type is recommended for use aboard small craft and is being adopted within the US.
SC 101	An earlier US standard below the requirement of Class D.

When buying a new radio, all that can be said at this stage is to make sure that the class of controller that's installed is a current type and that it will perform the functions you need.

DSC is changing the way we use marine VHF, MF and HF but is only one of the components that make up the GMDSS. Let's turn now to some of the others.

Inmarsat satellite communications

A principle difficulty with long distance MF/HF is that electromagnetic disturbances in the ionosphere can mean that there are occasionally times when communications are not possible. Satellite systems seldom have such difficulties, and provide better quality speech that's free from fading and have similar levels of privacy as land phone lines.

The Inmarsat (International Maritime Satellite) organisation is a private London-based company, responsible for worldwide mandatory satellite communications on SOLAS ships. It was the first provider of civil marine satellite communications services and operates a constellation of four geostationary satellites positioned at an altitude of 35,600km (22,120 miles) over the west and east Atlantic, Pacific and Indian Oceans as shown in Fig 3.3. Between them, they cover the globe between 70°N and 70°S.

The first Inmarsat system that became widely adopted is known as Standard A. It's an analogue system and is no longer being promoted. Also, due to its high cost and the space needed for the large dome housing its stabilised antenna, it is of limited interest to most small craft users. The replacement for Inmarsat-A is Inmarsat-B, which is a digital system offering high quality voice, telex, medium and high speed data and fax at generally lower prices. Like A, it is also recognised under the GMDSS and includes facilities for handling Distress, Urgency and Safety traffic though, again, the size of the antenna is too great for most small craft.

Inmarsat-C

Inmarsat-C is fully GMDSS compatible and therefore includes facilities for handling

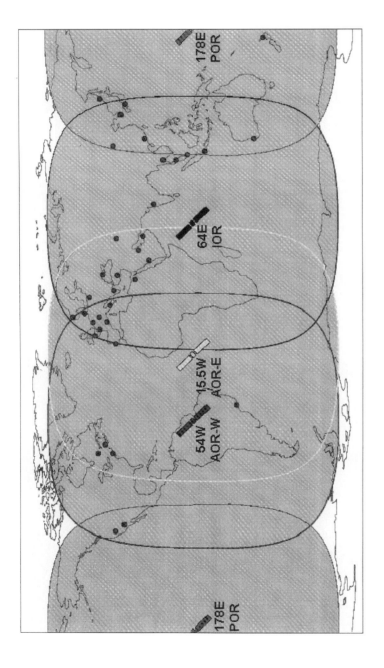

Fig 3.3 At an altitude of 35,600km above the equator, four Inmarsat geostationary satellites cover the world between 70°N and 70°S.

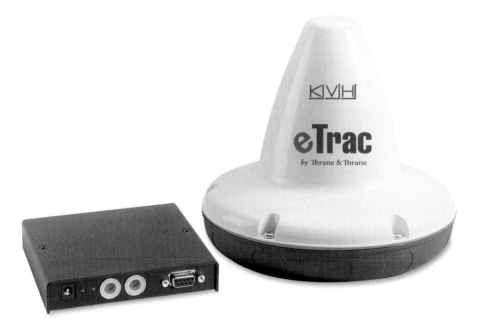

Fig 3.4 An Inmarsat-C antenna and electronics pack (courtesy of KVH Industries).

distress, safety and urgency messages. However, it is for data only and cannot handle voice messages. Compared to Inmarsats A and B, it is lower in cost, uses a compact omni-directional antenna the size of a pineapple (see Fig 3.4) and is extremely versatile. As a result, it is very popular with small craft users.

Inmarsat-C does not provide a direct data connection; instead messages are passed on a store and forward basis which means that delivery can be delayed for up to seven minutes. For full GMDSS compliance, there are restrictions on the type of computer terminals to which it can be connected, and much of the software in current use is non-GUI (Graphical User Interface) and reminiscent of that written for early MS DOS (Microsoft Disk Operating System). At 600bps, data rates by modern standards are slow, but more than adequate

for text e-mails and small file (<32Kb) transfers and, in spite of its shortcomings, Inmarsat-C has some interesting and useful features.

Enhanced Group Calling (EGC)

This is a service for delivering messages to multiple addresses. Messages include a special header that determines the area or administrative group of users that are to receive them. Two main types of EGC are FleetNET™ and SafetyNET™.

FleetNet™

This service is mainly of interest to commercial users or participants in a particular event. It enables delivery of messages of interest to fleets of vessels, eg company news, stock exchange reports, sports results, weather analyses and road or port information.

SafetyNet™

This is an international system for promulgating weather forecasts and warnings, navigational information and warning and other safety related messages. It is a service similar to Navtex (see p 44) and can be directed to individual vessels or vessels within a particular Navarea (see p 169) or defined geographical area. Those authorised to provide SafetyNET™ information include: hydrographic offices, meteorological offices, and rescue co-ordination centres.

Data reporting and polling

By connecting a data input to an Inmarsat-C terminal, the system can be configured to transmit values at specified time intervals. One example would be a GPS receiver that would enable the position of the vessel to be tracked automatically. Other inputs could include data from weather instruments or engine and cargo condition sensors.

Data polling is a similar process, but instead of transmitting the data at a specified time it is transmitted on demand by a shore station.

To make the most of these and other Inmarsat-C features, the terminal must be run continuously. Power requirements are quite modest but could be a prohibiting factor on sailing vessels with a tight power budget.

Fig 3.5 Inmarsat Fleet 77 (courtesy of KVH Industries).

Inmarsat Fleet F77

Inmarsat Fleet is a premium satellite service offering GMDSS compatibility, phone and broadband data. The data rates are a quantum leap in improvement over earlier services and, for the first time, give seafarers the ability to connect permanently to the internet at speeds that land users have long accepted as the norm. Users are able to choose between ISDN (Integrated Service Digital Network), giving speeds up to 64,000bps and pay for connected time, or MPD (Mobile Packet Data) where it is possible to stay permanently on line and pay only for the amount of data actually transferred.

Navtex

This international service is sponsored by the International Maritime Organisation (IMO) and provides mariners with MSI (Maritime Safety Information) text messages containing meteorological information, navigational warnings, urgent messages and search and rescue information. It is available in most parts of the world, though Australia and New Zealand are notable exceptions.

Information is collected from various sources by a Navtex co-ordinator and compilations are then sent, usually by telex, to appropriately located Navtex stations for transmission. The main frequency for transmission in English is 518kHz. Some countries transmit on 490kHz in local languages and for stations in GMDSS Areas A3 and A4 there is a further service on 4209.5kHz.

A dedicated Navtex receiver is usually a small device with few controls and a screen or printer for displaying received messages. They

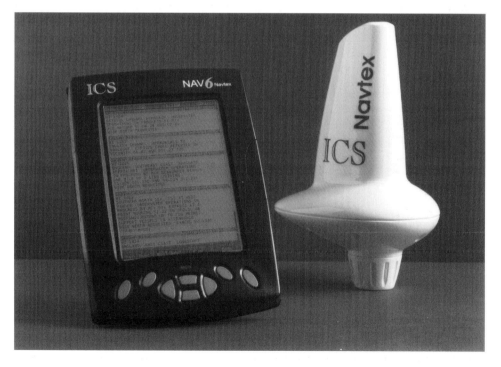

Fig 3.6 The ICS NAV6 Navtex receiver with antenna (courtesy of ICS Electroncis Ltd).

draw little power and are usually left to run continuously, displaying and storing messages as they are received.

Navtex broadcasts can also be received on a general purpose communications radio and decoded and displayed using a computer and sound card software (see Chapter 8). However, this arrangement has the disadvantage that the radio and computer cannot be left in a low power standby mode so that the

overall energy consumption will be higher than that of a dedicated, stand alone receiver.

The transmission and message format

To avoid interference, Navtex stations that are close to each other transmit at different times (see the schedule on page 150). Transmissions use a Telex On Radio (TOR) code known as

```
INSHORE WATERS FORECAST FOR THE UK ISSUED AT 0530
BST 19 AUGUST 2000
VALID FOR 24 HOURS

GENERAL SITUATION: A SLACK AREA OF LOW PRESURE
WILL AFFECT UNITED KINGDOM WATERS. A LOW IN THE
SOUTHWEST APPROACHES EXPECTED TO MOVE INTO THE
NORTH SEA AND DEEPEN AS IT MOVES AWAY
NORTHEASTWARDS.

FROM NORTH FORELAND TO ST.CATHERINE'S POINT
WIND: SOUTHWEST 4 OR 5, INCREASING 6 FOR A TIME.
WEATHER: SHOWERS.
VISIBILITY: MODERATE OR GOOD.
SEA STATE: MODERATE, OCCASIONALLY ROUGH.

FROM ST.CATHERINE'S POINT TO LANDS END.
WIND: WEST OR NORTHWEST 3 OR 4,OCCASIONALLY 5.
WEATHER: SHOWERS.
VISIBILITY: MODERATE OR GOOD.
SEA STATE: MODERATE.

OUTLOOK TILL (DAY 3) TUESDAY 22 AUGUST 2000
ATLANTIC LOW EXPECTED SOLE LATE ON MONDAY MOVING
INTO FASTNET ON TUESDAY, BRINGING STRONG SOUTHERLY
WINDS, BACKING EASTERLY LATER, TO THE SOUTHWEST
APPROACHES ON TUESDAY
```

A sample of a Navtex broadcast.

SITOR. This has been around for several decades and encodes characters as a sequence of audio frequency shifts. When heard on a standard receiver, it sounds something like a stone rattling in a car hubcap. The Navtex receiver has no loud speaker, but displays the decoded text on the screen or printer.

Navtex messages follow a standard format. First there is a preamble consisting of four character groups B1, B2, B3 & B4 which are coded as given below:

Navtex receiver features

Were the receiver to display every message received, users might find themselves overwhelmed by the amount of data, and types with printers may use unacceptable amounts of paper. This problem is overcome by logic within the unit that allows users to ignore certain types of messages. Navigational information, meteorological warnings and search and rescue messages cannot be turned off, but users may elect to reject other types if they feel they will be of no interest.

B1   Transmitter identification. This is a single letter identifying the station, eg F = Brest; L = Schevening; S = Niton.

B2   Subject identification. Another single letter used to identify the kind of message, as follows:

A   Coastal navigational information
B   Gale warning
C   Ice report
D   Search and rescue information
E   Meteorological forecasts
F   Pilot service message
G   Decca messages
H   Loran messages
I   Omega messages
J   Satnav messages
K   Other electronic nav aid messages
L   Additional navigational messages
V   Special services
W   Special services (possible other language use)
X   Special services
Y   Special services
Z   No messages on hand (QRU)

B3   Message numbering. These two characters form numbers within the range 01 to 99
&   and are used to identify particular messages within a subject group. After 99,
B4   numbering begins again at 01 and, to avoid the need to repeat any still in force, users are expected to have facilities for storing messages.

Emergency Position Indicating Radio Beacons (EPIRBs)

EPIRBs have been around for at least a couple of decades. They are self-contained radio devices that when activated send a distress signal. Internal batteries carry sufficient power to continue transmissions for a period of time between a few hours and several days or more. When received by a suitably equipped satellite or passing aircraft, the signal is relayed to an MRCC.

In 1979 a search and rescue satellite co-operation treaty was agreed between Canada, France, the then USSR and the US. Known as COSPAS/SARSAT, this led in 1980 to the establishment of an operational system of at least four polar orbiting satellites.

	COSPAS	SARSAT	Inmarsat
Controlled by	Russian Federation	United States – NOAA	Inmarsat
Spacecraft	NADEZHDA navigation satellite	NOAA weather satellite	Inmarsat
Orbit time (minutes)	105	100	Geostationary
Altitude (Km)	1000	850	35600
Inclination (°)	83	99	
Frequencies (MHz)	121.5, 406	121, 243, 406	1646 (L band) and optionally 121.5

Table 3.3 COSPAS/SARSAT satellite details.

EPIRBs come in a bewildering range of types and sizes with varying facilities and degrees of sophistication but are broadly classified as follows:

Class A	Operates on VHF-AM frequencies of 121.5 and 243MHz. These types are designed to be detected mainly by over-flying aircraft and have a nominal line of sight effective range. Activated by a manual switch, and by a hydrostatic release unit (HRU). Should the boat sink, the device is released at a predetermined depth and allowed to float to the surface and begin transmitting.
Class B	Same as Class A but for manual operation only.
Class S	Same as Class B but intended for survival craft use only.

> **Category 1**   Operates on 406.025MHz which is a dedicated satellite distress frequency monitored by COSPAS/SARSATS. Also includes a 121.5MHz homing signal and strobe light to assist in retrieval. The unit is designed to be both automatic float free and manually activated.
>
> **Category 2**   Essentially the same as Category 1 but for manual rather than float free operation.

The earliest class A or B types did no more than provide a signal from which the Doppler shift could be used to compute a position estimate. To relay the signal, a passing satellite needs to be in line of sight with both the EPIRB and ground station or LUT (Local User Terminal) at the same time. There are about 22 LUTs around the world but if this condition is not met, the message cannot be passed and as a result there are several parts of the world that are not covered. A further disadvantage is that the position can only be fixed to within a 10km (6 mile) radius, which in heavy seas can make small targets such as a liferaft or person difficult to spot. These types are still in use today and used mainly for coastal sailing and for small personal crew overboard beacons, where the 121.5MHz signal is used as a homing signal by search vessels and aircraft.

406 EPIRBs

Many of these early difficulties were overcome by the introduction of 406MHz EPIRBs. The two significant differences between these and previous types are that:

1 COSPAS/SARSAT satellites are equipped to store received EPIRB signal data and pass it to the next LUT that comes within range, thus giving coverage to the whole world.

2 EPIRB signals include a digital section which encodes details that include the user's MMSI and in some cases, like a DSC Distress Alert, may include a GPS position and an indication of the nature of the difficulties.

Just as with DSC radios, a 406 EPIRB is loaded with the MMSI of its parent vessel, which it transmits as part of its distress call. This is part of the registration procedure that is carried out when the unit is first purchased, which means that it should not be taken aboard another vessel or lent to another user. In some countries, the registration authority will accept a temporary change of details and may have a web site established for the purpose.

Hints to avoid false alarms

The false alarms that dogged the Class A and B EPIRBs can still occur, but at least with a 406 type and, as with DSC Distress Alerts, they cannot be made anonymously.

• Maintain and test your EPIRB in accordance with the manufacturer's instructions. Most types have a test facility that allows all circuits to be checked without generating a false alarm.
• Make sure that your beacon is correctly registered. If your contact details are on file

then should a false alarm occur a simple phone call may resolve the issue.

- Fix your registration sticker to the unit so that it can be easily read without taking the EPIRB from its bracket. False alarms have been generated by inspectors removing the unit from the bracket to read the label.
- Unless you are actually making a distress call, never remove the EPIRB from its bracket without first switching it off.
- Make a practice of making sure that your EPIRB is switched off whenever it is taken from the vessel.
- Keep in mind that activation of a 406MHz EPIRB for just a few seconds is likely to be detected and in a few minutes is likely to be located.
- If you should happen to trigger an EPIRB by mistake, some authorities advise switching it off immediately while others say it should be allowed to continue transmitting. In either case, it is important to contact any MRCC as quickly as possible to cancel the alert. If this can't be done directly then it should be passed via another vessel or shore station.

Enhancements

Many 406 EPIRBS are now also equipped to transmit a simultaneous distress signal on 121.5MHz and so can be detected by nearby aircraft. This is particularly useful for search aircraft, where direction-finding equipment can be used to home in on the casualty.

A further enhancement is the addition of a GPS receiver. This allows the unit to transmit its position to the satellite, giving an increase in fix accuracy and speed with which the details are relayed to the LUT.

Inmarsat-E EPIRBs

Inmarsat-E EPIRBs include an integral GPS receiver and have the advantage that their signals are always reported through at least two Coast Earth Stations (CES) and, with relay times of no more than a few seconds, a fast response is assured. However, since Inmarsat satellites are at an altitude some 36 times greater than COSPAS/SARSAT spacecraft, higher transmitter powers are required.

Search and Rescue Radar Transponders (SARTs)

Not to be confused with EPIRBs or simple radar reflectors, these are handheld active devices that make a distressed vessel or liferaft appear more conspicuous on the radar

	Class A or B	Bare 406 type	406 type with GPS	Inmarsat-E
Coverage (% of the world)	30	100	100	80
Reporting time	Up to 6 hours	45 minutes	4 minutes	2 to 5 minutes
Search radius (km)	20	2	0.01	0.01
Relative cost	1	6	7.5	12

Table 3.4 EPIRB performance summary.

screens of searching vessels or aircraft. They include a receiver which scans for X band radar signals and when detected they respond by transmitting a series of 12 pulses. On the screen of a searching radar set they produce a distinctive line of dots or arcs stretching about five miles away from the position of the SART. As the distance from the SART is decreased, the dots widen into arcs and then complete circles, as in Fig 3.7.

Handheld VHF sets

These can be an extremely useful item to have aboard a survival craft. Useful not only for contacting a passing vessel but also in directing rescue craft. Some lifeboats carry VHF direction finding equipment that can be used to home in on and locate a transmitter in a liferaft, even if it's not immediately visible.

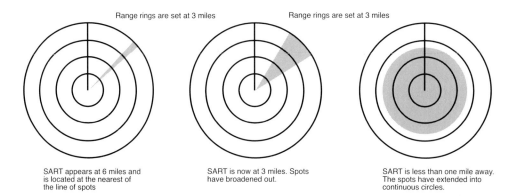

Range rings are set at 3 miles   Range rings are set at 3 miles

SART appears at 6 miles and is located at the nearest of the line of spots

SART is now at 3 miles. Spots have broadened out.

SART is less than one mile away. The spots have extended into continuous circles.

Fig 3.7 A radar view of a SART as range is decreased.

SARTs have a visible or audible indicator to show when they are switched on and an additional indicator to show when an interrogating radar signal has been detected. To maximise the chance of detection, they should be mounted as high as possible; clearly not easy in the case of a liferaft, though every little counts.

When the indicator is lying on the floor of a liferaft, a searching vessel whose radar scanner is at 15m (49 ft) above sea level has to be within about 1.8 miles to detect it. Simply holding the indicator upright increases this range to around 2.5 miles and raising it a further two metres increases the range to about 10 miles.

Clearly radios intended for this purpose must be ruggedly constructed. The GMDSS specification for handheld VHF sets includes water resistance to a depth of 1m (3ft) for five minutes, resistance to oil, and drops to a hard surface from a height of 1m. There are many other requirements but, in addition, it would be useful if they could be made to float, however this can be quite easily achieved by enclosing them in a plastic wallet.

Any handheld portable radio is only as good as its battery, and for emergency use these clearly need to have a long shelf life and high capacity; sufficient for at least eight hours of operation at high power is recommended. Some handhelds achieve power savings on standby by switching the receiver off for short periods when no signals are heard. It remains off for, say, 600ms, after which it is turned on for, say, 300ms. If signals are received it stays on but if not the cycle begins again.

As with the SART and other VHF, UHF devices, range is increased by increasing the antenna height. In a liferaft you can do little more than hold it as high as possible. If used aboard your main vessel, perhaps to cover the failure of a fixed radio, a considerable improvement in range could be achieved by replacing the handheld's antenna with a connection to the fixed radio antenna. To achieve this you will need appropriate connectors and adaptors, which are well worth obtaining and setting aside for this purpose.

Handheld VHF radios with DSC

These are available in the UK and are likely to become available elsewhere. Like other DSC VHF radios, when an alert is sent it includes the pre-programmed MMSI to identify the sender. Normally this would be the same as was issued to the parent vessel's ship's licence. With portable radios there is the strong possibility that they will from time to time be used aboard other vessels. In recognition of this, the UK have issued a special set of MMSIs for their exclusive use (see page 26), and a special 'Ship Portable Radio Licence'.

Narrow Band Direct Printing (NBDP) telex

NBDP is otherwise known as radio telex. It's an automated system of transmitting printable characters over MF/HF radio and has been

around for many years. It uses an error correcting code that exists in two forms – FEC (Forward Error Correction) and ARQ (Automatic Repeat Request). These and other technical aspects are covered in more detail in Chapter 8.

Vessels using NBDP are identified by their MMSI or Selcall number. This is a five-digit number which, like a callsign, is issued by the radio licensing authority and is encoded within the equipment. When, for example, a coast station initiates an ARQ call to a particular vessel, the vessel's Selcall is included, and when received, awakens the vessel's radio, which then switches from a passive listening mode to actively receiving the message that follows.

Although it is possible to use NBDP to carry out a one to one conversation with another person, communications are often fully automated, typically with the vessel station accessing a service provided by a coast station. In these cases, the vessel station may use codes to identify the service. For example, HELP+ gives a list of commands available; DIRTLXnnnnnn+ is a request for a direct telex connection with the number specified in nnnnnn and, if all else fails, OPR+ requests a direct contact with a human operator.

GMDSS: Strengths and weaknesses

As radio traffic levels increase, the introduction of DSC is helping to solve some of the major difficulties that have afflicted the traditional system of voice calling. To be sure that calls to your vessel are not missed, it is no longer necessary to listen all day to every other call between boats in your area. VHF has become more like a telephone where you only hear calls that are intended for you, and yet at the same time you can still receive safety messages of concern to all vessels in your area.

As a means of initiating distress calls, it also had great advantages. Provided that your radio has been properly installed and con-figured correctly, it takes little effort to make a distress call that includes all essential details: your position, identification and nature of the distress which is automatically repeated at four-minute intervals. Thus you are saved the need of having to repeat these details and given more time to deal with the emergency on hand.

Under marginal radio conditions, digital signals can often get through when analogue voice messages fail. Coast radio stations are frequently able to decode the digital part of a call but are unable to make contact on a voice channel. So for distress purposes it is extremely useful to be able to incorporate the essential details of the call within the DSC alert.

Ship to ship calls

To initiate any kind of DSC alert, it is necessary to have the MMSI of the station you intend to call. This is fine if you have already been given this information but if not how can it be found? Unfortunately there is no clear answer. Not all authorities have agreed to release this infor-mation. If they did, there is the question of how it would be accessed at sea. Sheer numbers rule out the possibility of a printed directory, and if prepared as a CD large numbers of craft without computers would be unable to use it.

For VHF, there is the option of using Channel 13, which under GMDSS is reserved

for 'bridge to bridge' communications. However, the call would need to be a voice call, which DSC was introduced to eliminate, and the called vessel would need to be monitoring Channel 13, which is only mandatory for SOLAS vessels.

The initial GMDSS concept

From its initial concept and planning, the GMDSS was intended to serve the needs of commercial vessels. The interests of small craft were barely considered and yet, in the UK alone, about 98 per cent of the 60,000 licensed vessels are leisure craft. As a result, and as use of the system by small craft has increased, many difficulties and anomalies have come to light. Most have been solved or worked around, though evolution is an ongoing process and it is certain that over the next few years there will be many changes in legislation and operating practice.

Acceptance of GMDSS around the world

While the UK and several other European countries have declared A1 coverage areas; have passed legislation to restrict the sale of radios that cannot support DSC, and have provided operator training courses, many other countries lag far behind.

In contrast, Australia and New Zealand have no Navtex service and No A1 or A2 coverage areas. At the time of writing, awareness of GMDSS amongst their sailing communities was low and there are no restrictions on the sale of non-DSC radios. The reasoning behind this approach is that both countries have search and rescue responsibilities for enormous parts of the

Indian and Pacific Oceans and see funding of these services as their main priority. Unlike Europe, they have long stretches of coastline with no existing VHF services so costs of establishing full A1 coverage would be high.

The USA and Canada lie between these two extremes, with large numbers of boats using the system but no formal requirement for operator training. Their approach is likely to rely more upon smart equipment rather than smart users, with the use of radios that include GPS modules as a first step and the way of overcoming the uncertainties of position reporting.

It is certain that for the years ahead there are going to be many changes to the GMDSS, particularly if we are to avoid the very real danger of a communications rift occurring between seafarers with and without DSC. The good news is that the requirement for SOLAS ships to keep a listening watch on Channel 16 is likely to continue. However, this provides breathing space only and all small craft sailors will need to be particularly watchful for changes in legislation, especially at critical times such as when buying new equipment or planning a voyage to other countries.

Chapter 4 • Amateur radio

'You know I have always considered myself an amateur' – Guglielmo Marconi

Don't be misled into thinking that the word 'amateur' in amateur radio means that it is in some way second rate. Many radio amateurs have, or have retired from, a professional interest in some aspect of the subject, perhaps as engineers or commercial operators.

Unlike CB or US Family radio, which operate on a small range of frequencies and with very low power, amateurs are free to use much higher powers and have access to bands in most parts of the radio spectrum. For small boats, it has very many benefits and privileges which more than justify the time and effort needed to obtain a licence and set up the necessary equipment. Where else would you find access to an e-mail service that really does work from anywhere in the world and is free?

Amateur radio resources

The Amateur Radio Service has been in existence from the very earliest days of radio and participants have often been instrumental in pushing ahead the boundaries of technology. The number of amateurs worldwide now runs into millions and, although licensing conditions are strict, it grants access to a wide range of frequencies stretching right across the radio spectrum. With such large numbers of participants, there is a wide spread of radio activities. Some are concerned with the pursuit of club awards, building satellite systems or emergency communications or just chatting to friends, but whatever activity it is, all have an equal right to their part of the band. Not all amateur activities are of interest to small craft operators but some are set up with the sole objective of providing a service to marine amateurs. In the next section, we look at a few examples.

Nets

These are like radio meeting places and can be a mine of information. Nets are frequencies and times at which groups of boats call in to report positions, enquire about the weather, marina charges, availability of spare parts or almost any topic of mutual interest. They are a way of obtaining first hand information on places you might visit and passing on your experiences to others following in your wake.

There are hundreds of nets operating throughout the world, many being ad hoc affairs that are started by small groups of amateurs that happen to be sailing together. Times and frequencies are arranged to suit themselves and the net may close down after a season or two. Others are more widely known, may have been established for many years and attract hundreds of listeners and active participants.

With so many callers, to keep order and avoid the mayhem of everyone calling at once, it is usual for one person to assume the key role of net controller. Their function is to allocate order to callers, and to try to arrange relay stations to help those with weaker signals that might otherwise be ignored. By no means all net controllers operate maritime stations themselves. Many are land based and are run by individuals who freely contribute huge amounts of their time and personal resources to helping small boats at sea. Often their professionalism matches that of commercial operators but their service is not something that should ever be taken for granted. They are, after all, amateurs who do what they do as a hobby, not because they are paid. It would be crass to assume that they will always be there or to make unfair demands. The success and character of nets depends very much upon the efforts of the net controllers, and the fact that around the world there are several nets that have operated regularly for ten or twenty years or more is a tribute to their efforts.

Maritime nets may be found operating on just about any of the amateur bands, though the SSB section of the 20 metre band is the most popular. 40 and 15 metre bands are close second favourites and have the advantage that they are often less busy. Exact frequencies and operating times of nets change too often for it to be possible to publish a full list of all nets though times and frequencies of some that have become well established are given in Part 2 (page 161). Once you have located a net, it's easy enough to call in and enquire about the operational details of others.

Slow Scan Television (SSTV)

Not like television as most people would understand the word, but a system for sending still colour or black and white pictures over HF radio. It's useful for exchanging digital camera shots, or scanned images between boats or shore stations. These could include pictures of anchorages, harbour approaches, chart or pilot book extracts, weather maps or just some shots of a happy crew.

A great thing about SSTV is that the equipment need not be expensive. In addition to a radio and a computer with a sound card, all that's needed is a cable to connect them together and some software that could be free (see Chapter 8).

Phone patches

This is a service that, due to licensing restrictions, is only available to US amateurs and other countries that have a Third Party Traffic agreement. Across the US many amateurs have set up equipment that allows them to connect their radio into the telephone system. Local calls within the US are free of charge and they are usually pleased to relay calls from other amateurs. When sailing in international waters, many US amateurs make frequent use of the service to make personal calls to friends and family at home.

E-mail services

Within the last couple of years, HF e-mail services have really taken off. Alongside the professional commercial providers there is one amateur service, WinLink 2000, whose mission statement is to:

Third party traffic

This is defined as a message received or sent on behalf of a non-amateur. It is forbidden in some countries though not in the US or between the following countries, with which it shares a Third Party Traffic agreement:

Antigua/	Costa Rica	Jamaica	St Vincent and
Barbuda	Cuba	Jordan	the Grenadines
Argentina	Dominican	Liberia	Sierra Leone
Australia	Republic	Marshall Islands	South Africa
Belize	Dominica	Mexico	Swaziland
Bolivia	Ecuador	Federated States	Trinidad &
Bosnia-	El Salvador	of Micronesia	Tobago
Herzegovina	Gambia	Nicaragua	Turkey
Brazil	Ghana	Panama	**United Kindom
Canada	Grenada	Paraguay	United States
Chile	Guatemala	Peru	Uruguay
Colombia	Guyana	Philippines	Venezuela
Federal Islamic	Haiti	*Pitcairn Island	
Republic of	Honduras	St Christopher & Nevis	
Comoros	Israel	St Lucia	

* From 1970 there has been an informal agreement allowing Pitcairn amateurs to exchange messages concerning medical emergencies, urgent need for equipment and supplies and private or personal matters of island residents.

** Limited to special event stations with callsign prefix GB (GB3 excluded).

'Provide a full-featured digital e-mail transfer, position reporting, weather, and bulletin service to the amateur radio community worldwide where internet access is not available.'

Development and growth are continuing rapidly, and in terms of numbers of users and technical sophistication the system far exceeds many of the commercial services.

An important requirement is that all correspondence must be covered not only by your own licensing conditions but also those of the US, because this is where the Central Mail server CMBO is located. US conditions prohibit communications in which either party has a pecuniary interest (Part 97.113 of FCC regulations revised in 1993). In effect this means that it is OK for you to send an e-mail to order a pizza provided that neither party works for the pizza company. Other countries forbid all commercial traffic.

For details of the hardware needed to use the service, see Chapter 8, and for more information on WinLink and how it compares with other e-mail services see Chapter 9.

*Ham Radio Aids Rescue on the High Seas

Amateur Radio operators again have assisted in a high seas rescue operation after pirates attacked a private sailing vessel on March 20 off Venezuela. The skipper, identified as Bo Altheden, reportedly was shot, and his female companion, ViVi-Maj Miren, summoned help via the Maritime Mobile Service Net on 20 meters. The victim was reported to be recovering in a Trinidad hospital.

According to Coast Guard Lt Jose Diaz, KP3J, of the Rescue Co-ordination Center in San Juan, Puerto Rico, the 44-foot ketch *Lorna*, of Swedish registry, was en route to Trinidad and Tobago when pirates attacked some three nautical miles offshore. Altheden was shot once in the abdomen.

The pirates destroyed the VHF radio, so Miren activated an emergency locator transmitter (ELT). The San Juan Rescue Co-ordination Center received ELT 'hits' from the *Lorna* and notified Venezuelan authorities.

Word arrived at Miami Coast Guard some 90 minutes later from the Maritime Mobile Service Net's Mike Pilgrim, K5MP, of a distress call from a woman on the *Lorna* on 14.300MHz. Miami Coast Guard forwarded the information to the San Juan rescue center. Diaz tuned to 14.300, where Bobby Graves, KB5HAV, Dave Dalziel, N4ICE, and Jim Hirschman, K4TCV – a physician who had assisted in an earlier rescue – already had activated an emergency net. An amateur in Trinidad, Eric Mackie, 9Z4CP, also assisted in communications.

Among those standing by on frequency were Ed Petzolt, K1LNC, in Florida, and Hector Godoy, HR3HGB, in Honduras, both of whom had experience of this type of rescue. The amateurs on 20 meters were able to calm the woman, and Hirschman provided medical counseling.

Diaz got permission from Venezuela to allow a vessel from Trinidad to assist, and a Venezuelan Navy vessel arrived on scene simultaneously with a Trinidad Coast Guard fast boat, with medical personnel. Trinidad medical personnel and crew took control of the sailboat from the shaken and exhausted Miren.

High seas made it too risky to move the victim. Instead, the Swedish sailboat continued on to Trinidad escorted by the Venezuelan Navy vessel and the Trinidad CG cutter.

Diaz credited amateurs with doing 'a tremendous job' in helping to keep Miren calm and to relay information for the US Coast Guard to her and for maintaining order on frequency.

'This is what it is all about,' Diaz said. 'Stay always ready, that others may live.' Pilgrim called the afternoon rescue 'one of the most rewarding experiences I have had during my 45 years on ham radio.'

*From ARRL Newsletter Vol. 20 No 12 23/March/2001

Fig 4.1 How long can amateur radio gear survive in a marine environment? This Yaesu FT757 was purchased second-hand over 20 years ago and is used daily for radio nets, e-mail and broadcast entertainment.

Amateur radio in an emergency

Amateur frequencies and transmission modes often seem to parallel similar services in the marine bands, but they can never match the integrity and reliability of professional services and the GMDSS. In the kind of emergency that presents an immediate threat to a vessel and or life, it would be totally wrong to expect amateur operators to be able to provide the most effective means of obtaining assistance. Responsibility for co-ordinating rescue effort is a duty performed by the Coastguard or military, and though exact arrangements differ between countries they usually have direct controlling access to other services such as lifeboats, search and rescue aircraft and other vessels in the area. Given most types of emergency, it's unlikely that one would find an amateur radio operator better placed to organise a rescue attempt.

With these points firmly in mind, there are, none the less, circumstances when amateur communications have been the only means of effecting a rescue but, for various reasons,

these are not always reported in the press. One such event that did get wide press coverage occurred during the BOC solo round the world challenge race in 1983. On the night of Wednesday 9 February, midway between New Zealand and Cape Horn, Jacques de Roux's 43ft boat *Skoiern III* was rolled. The Frenchman was saved from going overboard by a harness but was badly bruised and bleeding. The vessel righted itself but was in no fit state to continue although de Roux managed to raise the alarm via the Argos satellite transponder that was carried aboard. With this system, the vessel's position could be located to within five miles, but the problem was that there was no shipping in the area and the nearest land was 1800 miles away. The only possible source of help had to come from other competitors in the race. The task of contacting them was passed to Rhode Island amateur Rob Koziakowski. He was a disabled Vietnam war veteran who was operating from the basement of his house and had been in touch with competitors over the preceding weeks. He in turn passed the request to fellow amateurs and 12 hours later Matt Johnson on New Zealand's South Island managed to raise Richard Broadhead aboard *Perseverance of Medina*. He was some 300 miles beyond de Roux but none the less turned about for a rescue attempt. Under the conditions prevailing at the time, the return journey would take 40 hours or more. During this time, as more water was taken aboard *Skoiern III*, the situation became more desperate, and for Broadhead the job of finding de Roux was much like looking for a needle in a haystack. However both Koziakowski and Johnson were able to relay position information obtained from the Argos position indicators. Finally, at 19.39 on the Friday, the miracle happened and the two vessels made contact. Just five hours later the Argos on *Skoiern III* stopped transmitting, indicating that it had sunk.

In less remote parts of the earth, where rescue services are well established, amateur radio can still have a useful part to play, but in general its best use is not as a system of last resort but as a means of avoiding trouble before it happens. Not all emergencies happen quickly but more often as a sequence of minor events. In these cases, the radio can provide a means of obtaining advice or plain reassurance before circumstances deteriorate and become life threatening.

Calling MAYDAY or triggering an EPIRB tells the world that you are in distress, but sometimes, despite the situation being serious, it might not be that desperate just yet. An injured crew member or a damaged rudder both have the overall potential to threaten the safety of the boat but may not place it in immediate danger. In such cases, contact with another boat or one of the

maritime nets could be the easiest way of getting the advice needed or maybe averting premature rescue or salvage attempts.

Amateur radio without a licence

No one needs a licence to listen in to amateur transmissions. It's hard to know exactly how many listeners there are on the amateur nets but on the larger ones, especially those that give weather information, there is evidence to suggest that non-transmitting listeners occasionally outnumber licensed amateurs by several times. In addition to weather, it is often useful to keep in touch with the positions and intentions of other boats and to know that they have reached their destinations safely. Sadly, many people only discover the value of amateur radio after they have set off on an extended cruise. Once away from your home country, taking the necessary examinations and obtaining a licence becomes much more difficult.

Although anyone can buy amateur equipment, it must be emphasised that, other than in an emergency, without a licence it would be wrong to use it to transmit. A condition of the amateur licence is that except under clearly defined and exceptional circumstances, **radio amateurs are only permitted to pass messages to other licensed amateurs**.

From time to time licensing authorities take action against amateurs who infringe these conditions. Those who do so risk losing their licences, incurring fines and confiscation of their equipment. In the case of net controllers, this would not only be a loss to them as individuals, but also to the amateur radio and marine worlds as a whole.

Obtaining a licence

This is always easiest in your home country though many only discover the value of amateur radio after they've set out on an extended cruise and begin talking to others doing the same.

The procedure for obtaining a licence varies between countries and for specific details you are recommended to get in touch and join up with your national amateur radio society. The comments that follow outline broad similarities but, except when stated, are not aimed at anyone in particular.

Most countries issue two or three classes of licence. The first, Novice or B licence, usually gives access to parts of the VHF band and possibly low power use of a small number of HF frequencies. Higher classes grant greater privileges and allow the use of HF bands which are the ones of most interest to marine users. At each stage there is a written or multiple choice examination and for full access to HF there is at present a Morse code test.

It is at this point that many prospective amateurs lose hope and give up, which is unfortunate because in recent times the Morse requirements have been greatly

Is Morse code dead?

Certainly it is no longer recognised as an official means of communicating at sea, but dead? ... well, not quite. It still remains a requirement for full access to the HF amateur bands that are most valuable for long distance marine communications and has several unique advantages. Morse was the earliest method of modulating radio signals and can be used with the most primitive radio equipment. It is also a highly effective means of communication when radio conditions are difficult; when working with low power; a weak signal, or when trying to break through atmospheric noise and crackle.

Introduced by Samuel Morse in the 1830s, the code predates radio by half a century and at a subliminal level has infiltrated many facets of life today. Fragments live on in light and sound signals of the international code of signals, and occasionally it crops up in popular culture.

In the film *Independence Day* it was used by earthlings to confuse aliens, and in *Titanic* radio officers Jack Phillips and Harold Bride used it to summon the *Carpathia*.

In *Star Trek 5*, Scotty tapped out the words 'Stand back' to Spock and Kirk in a jail cell before he blew a hole in the wall to break them out.

During the second World War, the allied propaganda campaign connected the opening bars of Beethoven's 5th symphony with the Morse letter 'V', which became a subversive symbol for victory. Today the association is immortally engraved in the minds of many that were unborn at the time.

Morse remains a most intriguingly versatile method of communication. What other code can be sent by flashing lights, heliograph, on a conch shell, with flags, a whistle or the blinking of an eye?

relaxed, with the required speed dropping from 12 or 13 words per minute to just five. Special arrangements can usually be made for those with disabilities, and within the next few years the requirement for Morse may disappear completely.

Learning Morse

If you're teaching yourself, a Morse tutor software program (see page 169) is a good place to start. Start by learning the characters a few at a time by listening to them being sent at slow speed. Make a habit of writing down the characters you receive and when you feel confident that you've learnt the entire character set, try increasing the speed. Five-letter random groups are good traditional practice material; introduce figures and punctuation as you become more confident.

Some exams only test your ability to receive Morse, but learning to send is a fairly easy process once you've honed your receiving skills. Try to resist the temptation to begin sending until you are sure your receiving abilities are up to speed as bad habits learnt at an early stage are difficult to correct. If you are teaching yourself, it's hard to recognise your own idiosyncrasies, which others may find distracting and in extreme cases impossible to read. Even the best Morse practitioners develop an individual style or 'fist' that other trained operators find immediately recognisable.

Probably the most effective way of learning Morse is in company with others at an evening class. With a good teacher the subject becomes a pleasure rather than a drudge. Natural aptitudes for learning Morse are rare so don't expect to reach five words per minute in a

week but allow three to six months for comfortable progress. It takes no special gift to learn Morse, just determination and staying power but, like learning to ride a bike, once you've done it, the skill tends to stick.

The written/multiple choice exam

These are usually held at formal sessions once or twice a year and test knowledge of the regulations, operating practice and procedure and radio and electrical theory. Those already having some understanding of radio communications and electrical principles have a head start, especially for the first level exams, however it would be foolish to expect a walkover. No great depth of knowledge is required but if you have no prior experience, allow for about six months of one evening per week study. The standard is easily attainable by most enthusiastic individuals.

Obtaining a licence outside your home country

For some countries, where exams are administered once or twice a year by the national radio society, or an independent board, it may not be possible to take them in another country. For others, such as the British, it may be possible to make special arrangements through a consular office but there are additional fees and advanced bookings are essential. Arranging to take a Morse test in this way can be even more problematic.

The US ham licensing scheme

For an amateur radio qualification that can be taken by anyone of any nationality, anywhere in the world and at any time of the year, look no further than the US system. The only special requirement is that you provide a US mailing address to which your licence and any correspondence can be posted.

There are three grades of US licence: Technician, General and Extra and of these, for long distance HF marine use, the General is the minimum to strive for. Newcomers can take a single paper of 35 multiple choice questions and gain a Technician licence. Passing a five-word per minute Morse receiving test gives access to some HF frequencies, but passing a further 35 question paper gains you the General licence and access to the greater majority of the amateur spectrum. For those that feel like chasing what's left, the going gets tougher with a 50 question exam leading to the Extra grade license. Questions for each element are published both in exam primers and on the ARRL (Amateur Radio Relay League) web site.

The key part of the US exam system that makes it so user friendly is its army of volunteer examiners. To set up an exam test session, it has to be advertised in advance and there have to be a minimum of three examiners present. It can be held at any time and in any convenient location, even aboard a cruising boat. This happens regularly in several of the more popular cruising spots around the world, such as Neiafu in the Kingdom of Tonga, or the Bay of Islands, New Zealand. Depending how prepared you feel, you can take just the Technician written test and leave the rest to another day or, if the exam team are agreeable, take every element through to the Extra class at the same sitting.

Amateur callsigns

On passing your written exam, and Morse test if necessary, you can then go on to apply for a licence. This usually takes at least a few days and when granted you are allocated a callsign. You may have some degree of choice in your callsign and in special circumstances it may be changed later but once issued they usually remain with the licence holder indefinitely, upon payment of a regular renewal fee. Each callsign is unique but generally made up as follows:

1 or 2 characters + a single digit + up to 3 more characters.

The first characters are used to identify the country of issue, while the characters that follow may refer to a particular region within the country of issue, the class of licence and its date of issue.

Amateur stations are required to give their callsigns over the air at periodic intervals during transmissions. Their main purpose is as an aid to licence administrators and to help others identify sources of interference.

Reciprocal Licences

An amateur radio licence covers operation from within the borders of the issuing country and from international waters. When operating within other countries or within their territorial waters, it is necessary to hold a reciprocal licence from that country. The good news is that within recent years great efforts have been made towards unifying licence requirements and in countries that adopted the CEPT agreement, restrictions for bona fide visiting amateurs are minimal.

CEPT licences

Under a European agreement, a growing number of countries issue CEPT licences (European Conference of Postal and Telecommunications Administration). These enable amateurs to operate portable or mobile stations within countries that have implemented the CEPT Recommendation TR/61-01. The number of these countries is steadily increasing and at the time of writing (May 2002) includes:

Austria	Finland	Latvia	Portugal
Belgium	France	Liechtenstein	Romania
Bosnia & Herzegovina	Germany	Lithuania	Slovak Republic
Bulgaria	Greece	Luxembourg	South Africa
Canada	Hungary	Monaco	Spain
Croatia	Iceland	Netherlands	Sweden
Cyprus	Ireland	New Zealand	Switzerland
Czech Republic	Israel	Norway	Turkey
Denmark	Italy	Peru	USA
Estonia			

Amateurs taking advantage of these arrangements are required to operate within the terms and limitations in force both within their home country and the country that the licences are be used (those that are permitted in BOTH countries).

US amateurs

US amateurs may also operate in the following countries under their FCC licence.

American Samoa	Johnston Island	Northern	US Virgin Islands
Commonwealth of	Kure Island	Marianas Islands	Wake Island
Puerto Rico	Midway Island	Peale Island	Wilkes Island
Guam			

Most other countries offer a reciprocal licence and enquiries through their national radio society or radio communications authority will provide up to date information on what's needed. Some of the smaller island nations that receive large numbers of short-stay visitors see reciprocal licensing as a revenue earner and have little incentive for change.

Chapter 5 • **Communications alternatives**

'No matter how remote the location, you can have complete and secure access to e-mail and computer resources ...' (advertisement by *Clear Communications*)

If having an effective means of summoning help in an emergency is highest on your list of communications priorities, the obvious choice is to use GMDSS equipment for your area of operation, as described in the last chapter. However, the inclusion of new technology within the GMDSS is a slow process and greatly outpaced by commercial development. If your needs are also for general communications – weatherfax, satellite images, e-mail and internet data – it would be short-sighted to ignore the newer technologies. In some cases, for example mobile phones, land users form the target market, but the service is also useful at sea and economies of scale have meant that costs have plummeted. First, however, some words of warning.

The quotation at the head of this page was placed in the *New Zealand Net Guide*, a high profile magazine with a general readership but aimed at those with a higher than average understanding of technical issues. The message is so familiar and so often heard that it's a common belief that no matter where you go, easy phone, fax and internet services are sure to be available. In this particular case, the advertiser was promoting a product that used

a New Zealand cell phone network in a country in which there are vast areas of the land and territorial seas where cell phone coverage is marginal or non-existent. Following a complaint, the Advertising Standards Complaints Board later ruled that the advertisement was misleading and was to be withdrawn.

Had the advertisement used an Inmarsat phone (and for argument's sake we'll forget about submariners, underground workers, people in polar regions or lunar explorers), the claim of *'no matter how remote the location ...'* may have been sustainable, but even in this case the service is hugely more expensive than the norm for fixed phone lines, more difficult to repair and runs at a fraction of the speed for internet and e-mail data.

'Let the buyer beware' is the message, so choose your advisors with care. Good ones are becoming harder to find and as communications services become more complex, specialists in one branch of the technology may simply not have the time to keep abreast of developments in related fields. If you still need convincing, try asking a sales consultant at your local cell phone shop which sort of phone would be best for world marine travel. Can it be used from a 12 volt supply, what type of antenna would be best at sea, how would it work in sea areas around say the UK, USA, Spain or Australia? What would be the cost of calls and how would they be billed?

Citizen Band (CB) radio

Unlike marine or amateur radio, no examination passes are needed to use CB frequencies. In some countries a licence is required but formalities are minimal and for millions of people it has been an easy and attractive way of getting on the air. CB radio operates at frequencies around 27MHz and on the odd occasions, when conditions are favourable, quite large distances can be covered, though for most purposes ranges are unlikely to extend much beyond line of sight. In the United States, and many other countries where CB is permitted, it is transmitted as an AM signal, but in the UK and some western European countries FM is the standard, and

the use of imported AM equipment is forbidden. There are many groups of people for whom it fulfils a useful role, the best known being truck drivers, but in many towns and cities it is unfortunate that its popularity has led to overcrowding of the bands. Far more serious is the emergence of a small minority of mindless, moronic radio users, who devote their time to causing annoyance and disrupting the system. In areas in which they operate, these people effectively limit the usefulness of CB radio.

At sea, users are in a more advantageous position. Once away from population centres, activities on the bands decrease and as a means of chatting to friends CB does have a useful part to play. There are far fewer

Fig 5.1 Volunteer Marine Rescue Station VMR88, Bundaberg, Australia. Australia is the only country where, in addition to the usual international marine distress frequencies, rescue organisations routinely monitor CB radio bands. However, its use is declining.

restrictions attached to the use of CB than with the marine band frequencies. You can talk about almost anything (soliciting goods or services, transmission of offensive language or music are usually forbidden) and there are no restrictions on talking to shore-based stations.

Continuous Tone Coded Squelch System (CTCSS)

This is a feature that allows users to pick one of 38 sub-audible tones which, when applied to a particular channel, means that

> **CAUTION**
> Whilst CB can be useful at sea, it would be wrong to expect it to act as a substitute for marine band VHF. It is not monitored by ships, and with the exception of Australia, coastguard agencies may not be equipped to receive it.

Family Radio Service

This is a service that exists only in the US and Canada, though it is becoming increasingly popular, possibly because no licence is required and the radios are relatively inexpensive. In appearance, they are much like simplified marine VHF handhelds, but have 14 UHF channels beween 462 and 468MHz (see page 163). With an output power of half a watt the effective range of FRS is a few kilometres and is blocked by hills, buildings and other structures.

The main advantages of FRS radios are that there are no charges or restrictions. This means that it can be used for many purposes that are forbidden on other services, for example, con-versations between vessels and crew ashore

As FRS radios evolve, like mobile phones, manufacturers are adding more features. Some can be set to ring like a phone when incoming calls are on hand. One manufacturer's phones give a short beep ('roger beep') at the end of each transmission to indicate to the listener that it's now their turn to talk. Other FRS radios include broadcast band receivers, clocks and NOAA weather channels.

transmissions can only be heard by other users that have selected the same tone/channel combination. This provides a certain level of privacy, though when using it, it is as well to keep in mind that anyone listening in on a radio without CTCSS would hear the entire conversation.

Cellular phones

Many of the more popular cruising areas have excellent cell phone coverage. However, the phones become useless once they are taken much beyond line of sight of the nearest cell phone tower. None the less, because most cruising boats spend far more of their working life in sight of land than they do on passage, they are well worth considering for general phone calls, fax and data access.

A cell phone is also of no use unless it is supported by a billing agreement with a local phone company. Terms and conditions and charges for new phones, calls and service are in a constant state of flux as companies seek to respond to every nuance they detect in their customers' needs or competitors' weaknesses.

For users at the end of the line, it's a minefield of continually changing rules where the choices you make can have an enormous effect on the amount you pay for the service.

Before buying a phone and signing up with a cell phone company, be sure to ask for a list of other countries in which the phone can be used and whether foreign billing can be arranged. Vodafone, for example, offer a 'Global Roaming' service which, when set up, can enable you to use the phone from the moment you arrive. But whatever arrangement is on offer, be sure to read the small print or you may find you are paying international rates for calls received from your country of origin. If you anticipate staying in a country for a few months or more, it may be more cost effective to take out a new local contract. A search through the local providers' web sites will often give a list of their billing plans, conditions and coverage areas, but watch out for early termination penalties.

Data connections

Some phones include a small screen, keypad and functions that enable users to send and receive small e-mails and browse certain web sites. These are fine for viewing short text only weather forecasts but their size is a severe limitation for many applications. When viewing satellite images or synoptic charts, for example, fine detail is often important and a large screen essential.

Some cell phones have sockets for a cable connection to a computer where a dial-up connection to an ISP (Internet Service Provider) can give access to regular e-mail and web services. Unfortunately, there is no standard for connecting cell phones to computers and what works with one will not work with another. The interface may include a PCICMA card, infrared device, or an electronic unit that is in turn connected to the computer's serial port. In the Nokia 5110 phone shown in Fig 5.2, the connection is a simple cable that connects directly to the serial port.

Cell phone performance is undoubtedly improved with a higher external antenna but, to avoid signal loss, be sure to use the best quality cable. Some phones are designed specifically for marine installations; with separate antennas and higher output powers they can be expected to perform better in marginal signal areas.

For internet data, connection speeds are normally around the 9600bps mark though there are a couple of new technologies that promise improvements.

General Packet Radio Service (GPRS)

GPRS is a new technology that achieves more efficient transmission by breaking down information into discrete self-contained blocks or 'packets' and is used to deliver a higher speed data service over existing GSM networks. Advantages for users are:

• Higher data speed.
• You can remain on line paying only for data actually passed rather than connection time.
• While on line you can make and receive GSM phone calls.

To use GPRS you need a phone that's capable of using the service. Costs are considerably more than regular phones, but no doubt prices will fall when other faster technologies come on line.

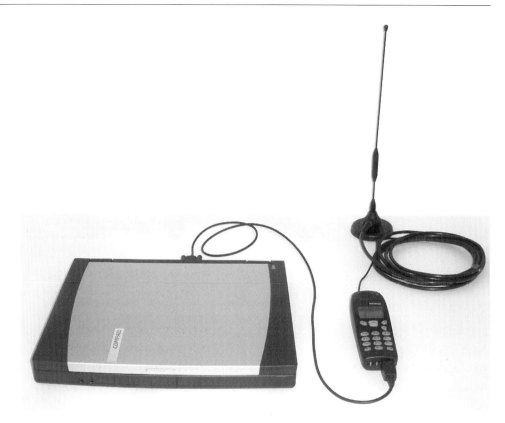

Fig 5.2 This Nokia cell phone connected to a Notebook computer provides a basic internet connection. The 'mag mount' remote antenna is intended for use on car roofs but is well sealed, made of non-corroding materials and has seen three years of continuous use aboard a sailing boat.

3rd Generation technology (3G)

Also known as UMTS (Universal Mobile Telecommunications System), 3rd Generation technology (3G) has been heralded by phone companies as 'the most exciting mobile development in years'. In some areas trials have been under way for some time. Its most significant benefit is an enormous increase in data transfer rates – up to 2,000,000bps is the figure often quoted. This will certainly pave the way for a far greater range of mobile phone applications, such as video conferencing.

Cell phone or marine VHF radio?

There is really no comparison, although it's a question that is often asked. When considering their use in an emergency the main advantages of marine VHF are:

- Distress and urgency calls are received by other vessels in the area, giving them the chance to respond if they are able to render assistance.
- With a masthead antenna, greater range can be achieved than with a cell phone held at deck level.

- Transmitted power is around 100 times greater than that of a cell phone.
- Some rescue vessels and aircraft carry direction-finding equipment that enables them to locate marine VHF transmitters. It's unlikely that they'll carry similar gear for cell phones.
- Coastguard and rescue services have trained operators and resources committed to responding to calls by marine radio. Telephone callers may find lines busy, or answered by a receptionist with no experience of handling distress traffic.
- There are no call charges.

Mobile satellite communications

Building, launching and maintaining a constellation of communications satellites is, to say the least, a costly business, usually affordable only by company consortiums or large multinationals. Plans have to be made several years before the hardware becomes operational, by which time market forecasts and regulatory requirements may have changed. Risks are high and sometimes a single satellite launch failure can have a big impact on the future of the enterprise. Returns on investment don't always make expectations either, as was demonstrated recently with the near collapse of the Iridium system after it was discovered that competition with terrestrial services (cellular and land line phones and radio systems) meant that consumers were just not prepared to pay quite so much for the convenience of a phone that worked anywhere.

When investing in a satellite phone, look not only at the hardware and its capabilities but also consider the company behind it.

During the lifetime of your phone, changes in their fortunes are certain to have a direct impact upon your own.

Globalstar

The current Globalstar constellation consists of 48 satellites plus four already in orbit as spares. At an altitude of 1.414km they are described as Low Earth Orbiting (LEO) satellites and are placed in eight orbital planes that are inclined at 52° to the equator with six satellites in each. Between them, they cover the entire globe between 70°N and 70°S although communications are only possible in particular parts of this region.

The GlobalStar system is described as 'bent pipe' communications in that signals to and from the user's phone are relayed by the satellite to a land based 'Gateway' station; a process which is only possible when the satellite has a direct view of both the user and the Gateway. At any given moment there are likely to be several satellites in view and when one that's in use passes out of sight, perhaps behind hills or buildings or over the horizon, the terrestrial Gateway is able to switch to another that is now better placed. In this way communications can be continued seamlessly as they move into and out of view. Very little signal processing is carried out aboard the satellites but is instead performed by ground stations that also carry out switching, monitoring and system control functions.

The Globalstar system provides telephone coverage in most continents and in sea areas within about 200 miles of the coast. Much of the world's oceans and polar regions are not covered. At the time of writing, Fig 5.3 gave an approximate indication of basic sea area cover-

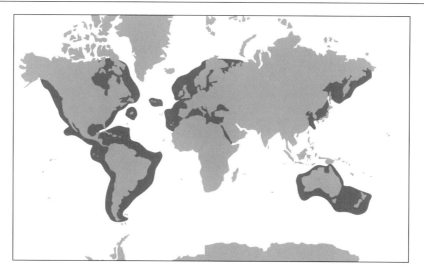

Fig 5.3 Globalstar basic sea area coverage (February 2002). Areas of 'Extended' cover are much greater and by the time that you read this, it is likely that coverage and services will be further improved.

Fig 5.4 Globalstar phone and antenna (courtesy of ICS Electronics Ltd).

age for phone and data services. However, the service is not spread equally in all areas. Use of a phone bought in one region may not be possible in others. In some areas there is no data service, yet in others fast Packet Switched service is available. As with most emerging communications technologies, there are frequent changes that are not always improvements and which may not be covered by published information. When making a decision to purchase, always seek confirmation from sales staff on current status and critical details.

Globalstar phones look and act like regular mobile phones. Since the satellites they are using are closer to the earth than geostationary satellites, the signal path is shorter and during phone conversations there is no obvious delay.

Iridium

Like Globalstar, the Iridium satellite system also uses LEOs satellites and gives high quality voice and data communications and is the only system that can cover the entire globe.

There are 66 working satellites in the Iridium constellation plus seven spares. They are located in near polar orbits at an altitude of 780km (485 miles) and take about 100 minutes to complete an orbit. Satellites are arranged in 11 orbital planes with six in each. Each satellite is able to exchange communications with ground stations and, unlike Globalstar, has four other neighbouring satellites, ie two in the same orbit and two in adjacent orbits.

Ground support systems consist of telephone Gateways, used to connect into the telephone system and the System Control

Fig 5.5 Iridium 9505 phone with attached antenna (courtesy of Iridium Satellite LLC).

Segment. This provides satellites with support and control services and Gateways with satellite tracking and message switching data. The primary cross links between satellites and the System Control Segment are via K-band feeders.

Iridium data services

A quick and handy feature is that anyone can send a free 120 character e-mail to any Iridium subscriber via their own e-mail or internet connection. When received, the phone beeps and the message is displayed on its screen.

A full data service is also available but, at a maximum speed of 2400bps is slower than many rival systems but fine for basic e-mail. Use Iridium to connect via your regular ISP and at this speed, general web browsing will be tediously slow. However, connect via Iridium's own web server and speeds four times faster are possible. This is achieved by compressing the transmitted data, and a small number of independent ISPs have also emerged offering this type of service for e-mail and web connections. Data compression can be beneficial, not just with Iridium but with other low bandwidth data connections such as HF cell phone or other satellite services.

Satellite tracking

Since Iridium satellites are polar orbiters, coverage is best near the poles where all orbital planes intersect, and worse in equatorial regions where satellites are spread more thinly. If you are closer to the equator than the poles and suffer occasional data dropouts, these may be occurring at times when the satellite you are using falls out of view and you are switched to another. To find out if this is the case, you will need to check the positions of satellites at the time of the dropout. To do this you will need their orbital data and a satellite tracking program. Details on how to obtain both of these items are available from the support web page for this book (www.pangolin.co.nz/radio/). For critical internet sessions, the Tracker will enable you to predict optimum times for use of satellites and thus minimise the chance of dropouts.

Inmarsat Mini-M

The Inmarsat organisation, with its firmly established mature satellite technology, has been around for many years. Although not part of the GMDSS, Inmarsat Mini-M offers high reliability phone, fax and 2400bps data.

Unlike the old Inmarsat-A, Mini-M uses a much smaller radome antenna, about the size

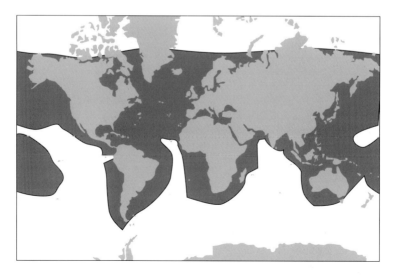

Fig 5.6 Approximate sea coverage of Inmarsat Mini-M.

Fig 5.7 Inmarsat Mini-M (courtesy of KVH Industries)

of a football and more suited to small craft. Using four primary geostationary satellites located at a distance of around 35,600km (22,120 miles) above the equator, Inmarsat-M gives good coverage of much of the globe but latitudes greater than 70° North and South and large areas of southern hemisphere oceans are excluded.

Inmarsat Fleet F77 and F55

Inmarsat Fleet 77 has already been described on page 34. The essential difference between it and F55 is that whereas F77 has GMDSS compliance and covers all latitudes between 70°N and 70°S, F55 is not compliant and has less comprehensive coverage. F55 equipment is also smaller and therefore more suited to small craft. However, both offer the same

broadband data services. Some of the possible applications of broadband data include:

• Automated chart updating direct from the relevant hydrographic agencies.
• Supply of the latest detailed meteorological charts and forecasts.
• Supply of pilotage and berthing information.
• Continuous position tracking.
• Real time e-mail.
• E-commerce – order spares and services before you reach port.
• Teleconferencing.
• Secure on-line business discussion.
• Remote engineering support.
• Remote medical support (telemedicine).

Provided reliability can be maintained, data services of this speed have the potential to

Summary of internet and e-mail connection methods

	Coverage	Equipment cost	Service cost	*Ease of use	Phone/ fax	E-mail	Web browsing	Possible speed (bps)
# HF (Commercial)	Worldwide	Medium	Low/ medium	2	Possible with some	Yes	Very limited	200 to 2400
# HF (Amateur)	Worldwide	Medium	Free	1	non commercial	non commercial	No	200 to 2400
Cell phone	Line of sight of phone tower	Low	Low/ medium	4	Yes	Yes	Yes	GSM 9600 CDMA 14400 GPRS 44000
Globalstar	See Fig 5.3	Medium	Medium	4	Yes	Yes	Yes	7200 sustained
Iridium	Worldwide	Medium	Medium	4	Yes	Yes	Slow	2400
Inmarsat-C	70°N to 70°S	Medium /high	Medium /high	3	Data only	Yes	No	600
Inmarsat-B	70°N to 70°S	High	High	4	Yes	Yes	Fast	64000
Inmarsat Mini-M	70°N to 70°S	High	High	4	Yes	Yes	Slow	2400
Inmarsat F77	70°N to 70°S	Highest	High	3	Yes	Yes	Fast	64000

See Chapter 8
*Ease of use scale: 1 to 5

make radical and far reaching changes to ways in which vessels are navigated and managed. By tradition, every vessel at sea is an independent entity, keeping its own copies of charts, pilot information, maintenance manuals, etc. The task of updating and correcting is becoming increasingly complex, time consuming and on the limits of the capabilities of many seafarers. Instead, it makes greater sense to leave suppliers of hydrographic information and marine equipment to update their own documentation and provide vessels with the ability to access it when needed.

Aboard my own boat, charts alone have long since spread beyond the space allowed by chart table drawers and take up much of a spare bunk. Many are years old and updating would be a formidable task. Instead, how much easier it would be to rent access to just the ones needed for the duration of the next voyage. Current pilotage details, weatherfax, weather routing and satellite images could also be drawn from the web. Have you ever entered a strange marina only to find that your impressions are quite different to the way it appeared on the chart or to find that your booked berth has been taken? Web cameras could provide a real time view of the approaches, showing other boats that are about to enter or leave and a real time view of visitors' berths.

Chapter 6 • Radio installation – demands made on the boat

Anyone who has ever installed a piece of equipment aboard a boat will know that it's seldom as easy as the sales information would have you believe. Often the difficulties have a kind of knock-on effect and you end up working on parts far removed from the original job. Communications installations are no exception and, apart from the mechanics of fitting units, transducers and running cables, any new item of equipment has some degree of impact on most other systems aboard, occasionally with effects that are far reaching and not immediately obvious. Manufacturers' instructions tend to focus on the needs of their particular product, but in this section we take a more holistic look of how communications equipment may affect and be affected by other equipment on board.

Finding the power

Although the initial energy may be provided by a wind generator, solar panel, alternator, etc, immediate power for virtually all onboard electrical equipment is derived from a battery. They are a key component of any boat's electrical system and fall into two categories: primary and secondary cells, ie non-rechargeables and rechargeables. Non-rechargeables are used extensively in portable equipment such as torches, radios, handheld GPS receivers and EPIRBs and are disposed of when exhausted. At one time zinc/carbon cells dominated the market, but now there are at least six different readily available types, and choosing the best for a particular purpose is a question of striking a balance between a variety of factors including cost, shelf life, charge capacity, maximum current drain, etc.

Primary cells

Zinc/carbon (Leclanché cells)

Available in standard sizes (see page 165) in a range of qualities and confusion of brand names. These cells are generally the least expensive and store the least energy but, as with other types, the exact amount they deliver depends very much upon how they are used.

Used to provide a heavy current (eg a transmitter, CD player or an electric shaver), they will deliver less total power than if used infrequently on a lighter load (eg a calculator or digital clock). A limitation here is their reduced shelf life and if they're left to expire in a radio, corrosive products may leak out and cause damage.

Zinc/chloride

Similar characteristics to zinc/carbon but with a slightly higher capacity. (For example Ever Ready Silver Seal)

Alkaline cells

These have virtually replaced the use of zinc cells in almost all applications and are the most common type available today. They contain up to four times the energy of zinc/carbon cells though, again, the exact amount will vary with the kind of load. Alkaline cells are well suited to applications where high currents are intermittently required (eg handheld transceivers, CD players, shavers). Recent types (Duracel M3) claim double the capacity of 'regular' alkaline cells, but at a higher price.

Lithium/iron disulphide

Available in AA size as a 1.5 volt cell offering extended life with high current loads and equal performance with low current loads. Weighs less than an equivalent alkaline cell, can be used at temperatures down to $-40°C$ and has a typical shelf life of ten years. Suitable for use with handheld transceivers, cameras, torches, etc.

Lithium/manganese dioxide

Available in PP3 and a few other sizes. Benefits are a flat voltage discharge characteristic throughout its life and even down to $-40°C$. Best suited to low current drain applications such as digital clocks and smoke detectors.

Lithium/thionyl chloride

Advantages of these cells are that they store a large amount of energy for their size and have very long shelf lives. Manufacturers predict ten years and during this time they are expected to lose only 1 per cent of their charge per year.

These lithium cells have a voltage of 3.7, which is different from that of zinc/carbon or alkaline types. They are also manufactured in a different range of sizes and are much more expensive. Generally, these cells are only used in equipment where they can be installed on a more or less permanent basis. (eg EPIRBs, distress beacons and in computers or transceivers, where they are used to provide memory backup power).

Secondary cells for portable equipment

Nickel/cadmium (Ni/Cd) batteries

These rechargeable cells come in all the familiar shapes and sizes of conventional zinc/carbon and alkaline cells, but in spite of a fairly high initial cost they can be an economic alternative for radios, torches and a whole variety of portable equipment used afloat. Their great advantage is that with a suitable charger and careful treatment, they can last for years and you have no need to carry stocks of disposables or worry about the problem of finding replacements.

At 1.25 volts per cell, their terminal voltage is slightly lower than that of disposable cells and this may cause problems with some voltage sensitive equipment. These are usually electronic items and if in doubt it is a good idea to check with the equipment manufacturers.

Characteristics of Ni/Cd cells are :

- Sturdy construction.
- Can be stored for long periods without deterioration or the need for periodic recharging.

- Relatively high self-discharge rate so cannot be stored for long periods in a charged state.
- Can deliver high currents.
- A life expectancy of 500 charge/discharge cycles is typical.

A characteristic of these batteries is their low internal resistance and this has several effects upon the way they are used. They should never be connected in parallel and if they are short circuited, excessive currents can flow causing internal heating and possibly serious damage. Apart from this, they are capable of delivering high currents and so are very suitable for loads such as portable transceivers, tape recorders, torches and electric shavers. Compared with other types of cells, they have a fairly high self-discharge (internal leakage) rate, which means that they are less suitable for electrical items that draw little current or stand idle for long periods. Examples here would be electric clocks, test meters and calculators and handheld transceivers.

Charging Ni/Cd batteries

Constant current charging is essential for Ni/Cd cells and the kind of battery chargers used for recharging lead acid batteries are unsuitable. Unfortunately, most chargers sold for Ni/Cd cells are designed to work from 110 or 240 volt AC mains supplies. This is fine if you are able to take them ashore for recharging, but afloat the most efficient method of charging is from the boat's DC power supply. Fig 6.1 gives a circuit diagram for a versatile charger that can be used to charge a variety of Ni/Cd cells from 12 volt supplies. Resistors R1 to R3 determine the output current and values can either be calculated or taken from the table on page 69.

Some types can withstand fast charging

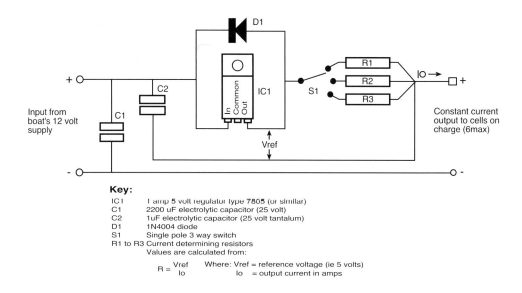

Fig. 6.1 Circuit diagram for a Ni/Cd battery charger, suitable for charging four cells in series.

Battery type	Values of R1, R2 & R3	Output current	Approx charge time
AA	82 ohms at 0.5 watts	60 mA	8 hours
C	22 ohms at 2.5 watts	227 mA	8 hours
D	10 ohms at 4.0 watts	500 mA	8 hours

Table 6.1 Resistance values for various maximum currents.

but you will need to check with the manufacturers for safe maximum current values and alter the resistance accordingly. When assembling the charger, the regulator IC should be bolted to a few square inches of copper or aluminium sheet to act as a heat sink. The resistors also dissipate a certain amount of heat and should be well ventilated.

The Ni/Cd memory effect

This is a problem that occurs when cells are habitually recharged before they are completely discharged. After charging, the terminal voltage falls quickly away and is particularly noticeable on loads such as computers, which are voltage sensitive. The solution is to make sure batteries are completely discharged before recharging. If not, subsequent charging as though they were flat is likely to cause damage through overcharging.

Nickel/metal hydride (Ni/Mh) batteries

These have similar performance characteristics to Ni/Cd cells but overcome the memory problem and are more expensive.

Lead acid batteries

Although normally associated with engine starting, lead acid batteries are also manufactured in much smaller sizes with either a gel electrolyte or liquid electrolyte that's held in place by a retentive separator.

Routine topping up with water is not needed and there is no acid spillage problem. They can be charged or discharged in any position and are well suited for use with portable equipment but are not manufactured in sizes that enable them to replace directly zinc/carbon or alkaline cells.

Charging is similar to methods used on other types of lead acid battery though they are more sensitive to overcharging, so the process needs to be monitored carefully and manufacturer's advice followed.

Main advantages for lead acid batteries are their relatively high capacity and low cost. A variety of types are available with characteristics suited for specific purposes such as cyclic recharging for portable transmitters or standby float charging in uninterruptible power supplies.

Power for permanently installed equipment

For marine engine starting, and powering all navigational, domestic and communications needs, there was once a choice between lead acid and alkaline (Ni/Fe or Ni/Cd) wet cells. Unfortunately, the great advantage of the latter – longevity – was outweighed by their high cost so now lead acids are used in virtually all marine installations. In all types the basic chemistry is similar. Negative plates are made from granular lead and positive plates from lead dioxide. On discharge, the acid strength weakens as some plate material is converted to lead sulphate, and on recharging the reaction is reversed. However, lead acid batteries can be constructed in several different ways, in different qualities, specifications, sizes and terminal configurations, so there is still plenty of room for choice.

Flooded batteries

These are the traditional types, constructed from lead mesh plates immersed in a sulphuric acid solution. Most easily available all over the world is the type used for engine starting. They are designed to deliver a large current for a short length of time and the engine's alternator immediately replenishes used charge. Used for this type of service they can last for years, but in installations where a large proportion of their capacity is used without fast recharging, their life expectancy is poor. Just one or two deep discharge cycles can be sufficient to ruin them. An alternative, more suited to marine power applications, are batteries specifically manufactured for deep discharge. These are constructed with fewer but thicker plates and can more easily withstand regular 50 to 70 per cent discharges.

All batteries within this group release small amounts of hydrogen during charging. As a result, they need to be well ventilated and care taken to avoid sparks by making sure that circuits are turned off when making or removing connections from the terminals, particularly after charging. Anyone who has ever witnessed a battery explosion, the shattered case and corrosive acid spray, will be clear on the need for caution.

Also, as a consequence of the hydrogen released, electrolyte levels need to be checked from time to time. If they fall more than 8mm below the level of the tops of the plates, topping up with distilled water (melted freezer frost) or de-ionised water is necessary.

When sulphuric acid is mixed with salt water, copious volumes of chlorine gas (an early chemical warfare agent) are released. A possible way for this to occur would be for a battery to break loose from its mountings in a heavy sea and for the case to become damaged as it crashes around the boat. To avoid the problem, great care must be taken to ensure that batteries are well secured, preferably by bolts. Strangely, provided the case and caps are undamaged, battery damage on sinking is not always as bad as one might expect. On several occasions, boats that have been quickly recovered after sinking and have had their engines flushed and oil replaced, have been started with energy still remaining in the battery.

Gel cells

These are similar to the gel cells described earlier but are larger. Hydrogen and oxygen produced during charging are recombined to make water so no topping up is either necessary or possible. In case of overcharging, a pressure relief valve is fitted to vent off any excess gas though battery life is then affected.

Absorbent Glass Mat (AGM) batteries

Plates in these batteries are separated by a pad of fibreglass mat, giving a very dense and strong construction. During manufacture it is saturated with a measured volume of electro-

	Flooded	Gel	AGM
Safety	Hydrogen must be allowed to escape. Care needed to avoid sparks and spilt acid	No possibility of leaks even when inverted	No possibility o leaks even when inverted
Charging	Less susceptible to overcharging	Requires careful control	Requires careful control
Maintenance	Routine checks on electrolyte levels, also regular recharging during periods of disuse	External cleaning only	External cleaning only
Approximate self-discharge rate per month	6.5%	3%	3%
Life expectancy	From days to years depending on treatment	Over 500 full charge/discharge cycles are typical	Over 500 full charge/discharge cycles are typical
Other features	Charge condition can be checked with a hydrometer. Low weight per ampere hour	Good low temperature performance	Can be used for deep cycle or engine starting
Availability	Most parts of the world	Only from certain suppliers	Only from certain suppliers
Comparative costs	1	2 to 3	2 to 3

Table 6.2 Lead acid battery comparison.

lyte, which cannot be topped up or replaced during the life of the battery. Provisions are made to recombine gases produced during the charging process, so under normal conditions there is no escape to the atmosphere.

Finding the energy

The distinction between power and energy is important but sometimes missed. An engine starter motor has lots of *power*; in the region of 6kw or 8 horsepower, but a typical engine starting battery only has enough *energy* to run it for a minute or so. *Power* is measured in watts and is the result of voltage multiplied by current. *Energy* is measured in joules and is the result of *power* (watts) multiplied by time (seconds) or, in other words, the length of time for which an electrical item can be kept running – staying power.

Aboard most small craft, this is a crucial factor as most loads, eg GPS and navigation lights, are quite small but often used continuously for many hours and perhaps the whole duration of a voyage. So power requirement is quite modest but total energy requirement is considerable. As a guide, Table 6.3 gives a list of current requirements for some commonly installed items.

A boat battery is like a bank account for storing energy and ultimately all that you use has to be replaced by some form of charging: running an alternator, solar, wind or shore power. Unfortunately, there is no easy equivalent of the bank statement; no simple fuel gauge that you can quickly check to see how much you have left, and the more crew you

have aboard, the greater the difficulty in keeping a mental tally.

Clearly, it is important to have some idea of the state of charge of your batteries, if only to be assured that you'll be able to start the engine when it's next needed. With flooded cells, the easiest and most reliable method is to use a hydrometer: a simple calibrated float that measures the specific gravity of the electrolyte. A higher specific gravity means that the acid is more concentrated and the battery more charged. Fig 6.2 shows the relationship between specific gravity and state of charge.

A hydrometer is of no use with gel or AGM batteries, but another indicator of the state of charge can be obtained by measuring the off load voltage between the terminals. A digital

Equipment	Current (amps)
100 watt HF transceiver	2 on receive. 19 on transmit*
25 watt Marine VHF with DSC (ICS)	0.3 on receive. 0.18 on standby. 5.5 when transmitting at 25 watts. 1.3 when transmitting at 1 watt. 0.18 standby.
Handheld VHF radio	0.019 on standby. 0.15 when receiving. 1.5 when transmitting.
Mini-M satellite phone	2.08 on standby. 3.3 when used for phone calls. 4.16 when used for fax or data.
Notebook computer	Typically 0.8 to 2.5 depending on what accessories are running.
KAM multimode decoder	<0.3
PK-232 decoder	0.7
MFJ decoder	0.4
Pactor 2 modem PTC IIe	0.5

*Note: *This is a maximum value and occurs when transmitting data or on speech peaks. Mean consumption when transmitting SSB voice is considerably lower.*

Table 6.3 Typical current demands for 12 volt communications equipment.

rather than analogue voltmeter is best for this purpose and again Fig 6.2 shows the relationship.

Another device that's useful in keeping track of battery energy is a digital current meter. For this purpose, it's connected in series with one of the battery cables and must be able to carry the maximum current required for engine starters, anchor winches, etc and yet be able to resolve milliamps. A range of 0.001 to 999 amps would be ideal for most applications and give an instant reading of the net balance between charge current and current being consumed by equipment in use. With everything switched off it can also provide a useful indication of a leakage that may require investigation.

A further convenience would be to install an energy monitoring unit. In addition to simply measuring instantaneous net current, these units include an internal computer and memory to record voltage and net charge over a period of time. By following trends they are able to measure battery efficiency and compute the amount of charge remaining at any time.

Voltage compatibility

Thankfully, most boats use 12 volt electrical systems. This is a standard inherited from the road vehicle industry and is responsible for

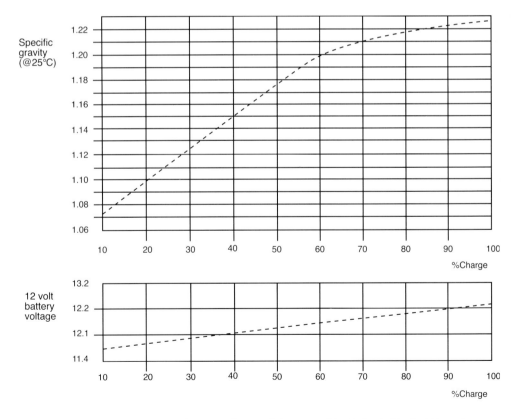

Fig 6.2 Specific gravity and battery voltage as indicators of charge condition in flooded lead acid batteries.

the emergence of the huge range of equipment manufactured for this voltage. Some larger boats follow commercial vehicle standards and have 24 volts. This does have the advantage of needing smaller cables to conduct the same power, but users may find it harder to obtain electrical accessories, particularly away from the more industrialised areas.

Countless millions of road vehicles with 12 volt electrical systems all produce electricity from engine driven alternators and use lead acid batteries for storage. A characteristic of these batteries is that though they are nominally rated at 12 volts, their terminal voltage may rise to 15 volts when they are under charge, or fall to 11 volts when they are flat. Most equipment intended to operate in vehicles or on 12 volt marine systems, is manufactured to cope with these fluctuations, but in the case of items not primarily intended for mobile use, a check on voltage compatibility is essential.

Voltage fluctuations in marine systems, sailing boats in particular, are often greater than those found in vehicles. This is because small loads such as cabin or navigation lights are often run for long periods without the engine running, thus pulling the voltage down to a lower level. Many SSB transceivers are sensitive to low voltage and although the receiver may appear to function correctly, the transmitted signal is distorted. If the battery can't provide the power needed, the transmitter shuts down on speech peaks, producing characteristically 'clipped' speech, where loud parts of the voice are missing.

At some stage, you are sure to need to run a piece of equipment that's designed for a supply other than 12 volt DC: perhaps a computer, power tool, or domestic appliance.

Converting to another voltage will inevitably lead to losses so it is as well to examine your options before pressing ahead. These include the use of resistive or switching regulators or an inverter and are available from electronics stores and better equipped marine suppliers in a range of voltages and currents.

Resistive regulators

These can only provide a lower voltage and usually at not more than a couple of amps. Essentially, they consist of an electronically variable resistor connected in series with the power supply. The resistor may be a power transistor with a control circuit that alters its resistance in such a way that the output voltage remains constant irrespective of the current drawn. Losses will be lower if the difference between input and output voltages is small and if the current drawn is low. As such, resistive regulators are a good choice for small radio receivers, clocks or mobile phones.

Switching regulators

These are available in types that can 'step up' or 'step down' the supply voltage. Their working principle is similar to that of an inverter (see below), where the supply is converted to an alternating wave form, then 'transformed' to the required voltage and then rectified back to DC. They are generally designed for higher currents than resistive regulators, are more efficient and more expensive. They have the potential to produce electrical interference but on better quality designs this is reduced to an acceptable level.

Inverters

Inverters are electronic devices that convert low voltage DC to higher voltage AC. Tiny ones

Battery voltage range	10–15.5VDC (12 volt model)
	20.0–31.0VDC (24 volt model)
Battery cut out	10.0VDC (12 volt model)
	20.0VDC (24 volt model)
Frequency regulation	0.005% @ 50Hz
Output power (continuous)	2000VA
Output power (15 seconds)	4500VA
Voltage regulation	5% True RMS
Output voltage	230VAC
Wave form	Modified Sine Wave
Power factors allowed	All
Full load efficiency	84%
Peak efficiency	93%
No load drain	0.12 amp
Dimensions	305mm x 292mm x 222mm
Weight	23.6kg

Table 6.4 Specification extract for the Heart Freedom 2000 inverter charger.

are included in 12 volt fluorescent strip lights but the term is usually applied to higher power units that convert battery power to 110 or 230/240 volt AC at 60 or 50Hz. They are a very convenient way of running most domestic appliances from the boat's supply, though there are of course inefficiencies. Most manufacturers make these clear in their specification and, as an example, Table 6.4 shows a summary of details for the Heart Freedom 2000, which is also able to act as a battery charger when shore power is available.

Inverters can also be a source of radio interference, with some far worse in this respect than others. In their current models, most reputable manufacturers take care to limit its effect but in other cases, once installed, it can be very difficult for users to eliminate.

Radio interference

Natural sources of radio interference include thunderstorms and atmospheric static but, apart from disconnecting the antenna, there's little that can be done to reduce them. This also applies to most man-made sources outside the boat, but where interference is a problem, onboard sources are a common cause, if only because they are closer.

Interference can be a serious and, occasionally, elusive problem and can affect not only communications equipment but also autopilots, computers, depth sounders; in fact almost any piece of electronic gear. When planning new installations, its avoidance is sometimes given little thought until its harmful effects become too obvious to be ignored. These can be quite varied but may include any of the following:

- Noisy radio reception over a wide band of frequencies
- Radio reception on single frequency is noisy or absent
- Depth sounders show false readings
- Weatherfax pictures become cluttered by patterns or odd marks
- Radar displays show sudden bright lines*
- Autopilots behave erratically*
- Electronic navigational data is corrupted*

Onboard transmitters are the usual cause of these effects.

In searching for the source, begin by progressively and systematically turning off parts of the electrical system whilst listening to the interference and noting any change. The following list includes some common sources:

a) Alternators
b) Any form of electric spark (eg ignition systems on gas or diesel heaters, outboards or generators)
c) Computers and other digital equipment
d) Dynamos, wind generators or electric motors
e) Echo sounders
f) Power inverters – including types fitted to low voltage fluorescent strip lights
g) Mains voltage dimmers and electronic motor speed controllers, eg as fitted to sewing machines
h) Radar sets
i) Shore power connections
j) Switches, thermostats and relay contacts
k) Loose or bad electrical connections
l) Electrolytic corrosion between dissimilar metals, eg corroding cable connection, rusting bolts
m) Rotating parts of propeller shafts

Should your initial check fail to locate the trouble, then running the affected radio from a temporary set of leads connected directly to an isolated battery is the next step. If the interference is eliminated then a thorough check of the electrical system for bad connections is called for.

In some cases the source of interference will be obvious and if you are lucky it may be cured by simply moving the equipment around. If unlucky, tracking it down will require a careful and logical inspection of the boat's entire electrical system and in the case of k, l, and m above, maybe even mechanical and underwater parts as well.

Most difficult to locate is interference that still persists when all electrical equipment is turned off and the main batteries isolated. The cause is most likely to be due to small electrolytic currents produced by wet dissimilar metals. Try looking for the source by moving the affected equipment to find the position in which interference is strongest. If it is below the waterline it may disappear after hauling out and a thorough drying.

Once you have located a source, the next question is what to do about it and, to help understand more of the problem, it is useful to divide interference into two types – connected interference (ie passed through power and connecting cables) and radiated interference.

Connected interference

This occurs as a small fluctuating voltage superimposed upon the vessel's DC power supply and becomes troublesome if picked up and amplified by radio equipment (see Fig 6.3).

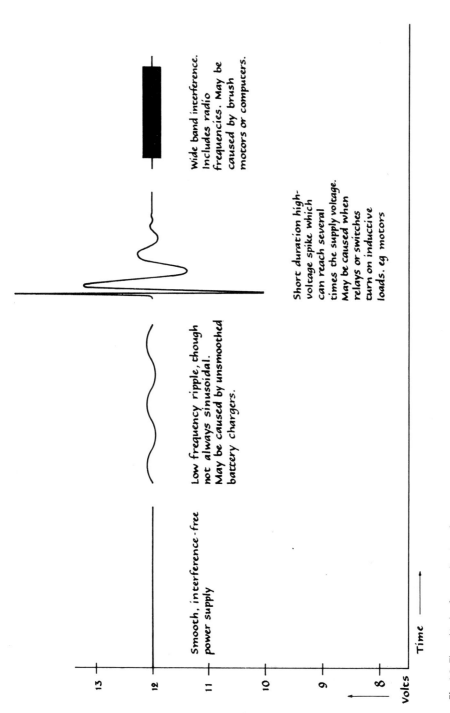

Fig 6.3 Three kinds of power line interference.

Low frequency ripple

Battery chargers with unsmoothed outputs are a common cause of this kind of interference which, with 50Hz mains, may appear as a distinctive 100Hz tone in radio loudspeakers. Smoothing components usually include a large value electrolytic capacitor (several thousand micro farads) connected across the charger output and possibly a series choke, but these components are not always included. On cheaper chargers they are left out for economic reasons, but on some more expensive electronic types they are left out for design reasons. In the latter case, adding these components will affect charge regulation. Wind generators can produce a similar effect, but the tone frequency will vary with wind speed.

With transceivers, be aware that even if received signals sound clear and interference free, the same may not be true of the transmitted signal. When transmitting, the transceiver draws more current and uses different circuits. In this case, to detect the problem you will need to carry out a test transmission and get a signal report from another station. In one example of this problem, where the interference was caused by a wind generator, the signal was only affected during wind gusts when the received signal was obliterated by noise.

High voltage spikes (transients)

High voltage spikes may be produced when inductive loads (eg pumps, motors, relays, solenoids, coils, etc.) are switched on or off and, although they may be extremely short-lived, they can be extremely damaging to unprotected electronic equipment. Failures from this cause can be especially troublesome to track down as the effects are so brief,

require specialist equipment to observe, and are often difficult to reproduce. Fortunately, manufacturers of better quality marine electronics are well aware of just how electrically noisy boat electrical systems can be and their potential for damage. As a result most marine equipment on sale today includes spike suppression, but this may not be the true for equipment sold for other markets.

Even if high voltage transients are not a noticeable problem, some simple precautions to minimise transients are good practice and could avert a premature equipment failure. These include:

• Replacing brush gear on electric motors or dynamos before wear causes arcing and commutator damage.
• Fit a capacitor and resistor across switch contacts that control inductive loads (see Fig 6.4). Pressure and float switches used to control water pumps and relays controlling autopilot helm motors all benefit from this treatment, which also extends switch contact life.

Radiated interference

Some types of interference are not constrained by connecting wires but pass freely into space like other kinds of radio transmissions. The connecting leads of equipment producing radio frequency interference act as antennas, thus allowing it to affect equipment some distance away. Often the noise is transferred between cables that run within the same ducting but it may also be picked up by other metal items (eg standing rigging, metal window frames, etc) and re-radiated into space. This characteristic adds further to the difficulties of locating the source of the interference.

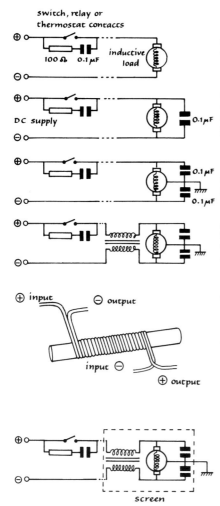

switch, relay or
thermostat contacts

Connecting a 100Ω resistor and 0.1 μF capacitor across switch contacts helps prolong switch life and eliminate interference.

Connecting a capacitor across noisy electrical equipment may eliminate interference. You may need to experiment with different values for higher frequencies.

If one capacitor doesn't work, try a pair of the same value. Connect the junction and the equipment case (if it is metal) to an effective earth.

A pair of chokes connected in series with the power supply can also be effective in blocking interference. These are available commercially or can be home made.

Chokes can be made by winding a pair of wires around a ferrite rod. Use enamel insulated wire of the type used in electric motor windings. Ferrite rods can be obtained from scrap portable radios where they are used in the antenna. Begin by wrapping a few turns of brown paper tape around the rod, then close wind the pair of wires and secure them in place. Finish with a coat of varnish or clear epoxy and connect up as shown.

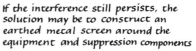

If the interference still persists, the solution may be to construct an earthed metal screen around the equipment and suppression components

Fig 6.4 Methods of reducing interference.

This radio frequency noise can be produced in a variety of ways but aboard boats the most likely sources are:

• Any kind of electric sparks, such as can be produced by electric motor/dynamo brushes, bells, buzzers or ignition systems.
• Any kind of equipment in which currents are rapidly switched, eg alternators, power inverters and digital equipment such as computers.

On installing new equipment, the possibilities for interference can be reduced by taking care over the kind of cables that are used and the way in which they are laid:

1 Use screened cable for any interconnections to decoders, computers and accessories and make sure that the screen is grounded at one end of the run. Grounding at both ends is not always a good idea as noise may be picked up by the loop that this creates.

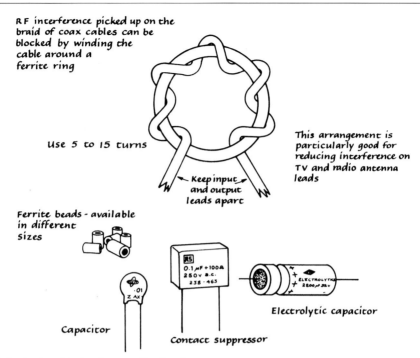

RF interference picked up on the braid of coax cables can be blocked by winding the cable around a ferrite ring

Use 5 to 15 turns

This arrangement is particularly good for reducing interference on TV and radio antenna leads

Keep input and output leads apart

Ferrite beads - available in different sizes

.01
Z AX

A5
0.1 µF + 100A
250V a.c.
238 · 463

ELECTROLYTIC
2200µ 35v

Electrolytic capacitor

Capacitor

Contact suppressor

Fig 6.5 A selection of devices for controlling interference.

2 Try to ensure that the positive and negative conductors (or, in the case of AC circuits, live and neutral) of each individual circuit are kept close together and not routed separately.

3 Try to keep any HF transceiver wiring away from wiring for autopilots or electronic navigational equipment such as electronic navigators or chart plotters.

4 Make all interconnections as short as possible.

5 Try to keep antenna runs away from equipment control lines and/or interconnecting wires. If they need to cross, they should do so at an angle near 90 degrees. Ground leads should be as short as possible and earthing must be effective.

Dealing with this kind of interference once it has become a problem is often a case of trial and error. What works in one set of circumstances may not work in another, but occasionally simply resiting the affected equipment makes the difficulties go away. Fig 6.5 gives more general ideas for tackling radio frequency interference.

Avoiding interference to other radio users

With any radio transmission there is no guarantee that it will only be picked up by equipment designed to receive it. There have been several well reported cases of strong signals received on bed frames and similar structures, where the spring mesh acts as an antenna and a rusty bolt the detector. More common are other radio users that suffer interference from transmitters operating on frequencies some distance away from those on which their receivers are tuned. The cause

Noisy Computers

Electrical noise in computers can be especially troublesome if the computer is to be used with a radio for receiving weatherfax, satellite images or e-mail. Fortunately, manufacturers are aware of the difficulties and have to comply with fairly stringent standards for the elimination of interference. However, it still occurs from time to time and in dealing with the problem some points to check (listed in order) are as follows:

- Use screened cables for all interconnections and make sure that one end of the screen is connected to an effective earth.
- Thread ferrite beads along leads at the point of entry to the computer.
- Try moving the computer. Using it on the other side of a metal bulkhead may provide sufficient screening.
- Try constructing an earthed metal screen around the computer. Experiment with cooking foil first to see if the idea works.

may be bad design or maladjustment in either transmitter or receiver but even perfectly adjusted transmitters can occasionally produce signals that 'break through' on other electrical equipment, particularly if it is close by. At sea, such problems are less likely to occur but in close proximity to others, say in a marina, this situation is quite different. In these situations the ship radio licence only allows marine band calls to be made to port operations and similar services. However, in the absence of any local restrictions, the use of CB or amateur frequencies may be allowed, and if these are used it is important to take steps to avoid interfering with other radio users, and emergency services in particular.

Exceptionally strong radio signals can affect almost any kind of electrical equipment but perhaps most complaints arising from 'break through' are from users of domestic radios or television sets. In these cases, there is no doubt that some (especially older) sets are unduly sensitive to strong, off frequency signals, and it is a difficulty that recently adopted manufacturing standards have done much to relieve. None the less, even if the neighbour's TV set is unreasonably sensitive and picks up noise from every car or outboard that passes, if your transmissions blot out their favourite evening's viewing, it could be hard to convince them that it is their set that is at fault.

Practical solutions to these problems often lie in a tactful and diplomatic attitude rather than in changes to equipment. By adopting good practices in installation and operation, such difficulties are less likely to occur.

For example :

a) Ground the cases of all equipment that handle RF.
b) Use short, direct ground leads.
c) Use of braid breakers and toroids can help eliminate RF on the outside of coax screens.
d) Once you have established a contact,

reduce transmitter power to the minimum needed to maintain it.

e) Disconnect any shore power connection and run on the boat's batteries whilst transmitting.

Protection against lightning

Lightning strikes pass currents of around 2000 to 200,000 amperes and although of only short duration, can still cause dangerous heating effects in the materials through which it passes. If these are poorly connected metal parts or indifferent insulators, such as wet wood, the result can be explosive and cause fires. Also, because of large magnetic effects associated with currents of this size, fields within the boat will be substantially altered and even if the compass itself is unaffected, its deviation may be radically changed. Other magnetic effects might include the erasure of cassette tapes and computer disk memory.

The probability of being struck by lightning varies considerably in different parts of the world but its effects are so devastating that provisions to limit its damage to the boat as a whole are a sensible precaution. However, this section is concerned only with its effects upon radio equipment.

As far as radio equipment is concerned, it does not require a direct strike to cause considerable damage. Insulated metalwork such as antennas can acquire high voltages from static charges or strikes close by. Not only are these likely to damage any equipment to which they are connected but are also a danger to anyone touching them. In addition, on wooden or plastic hulls there is also an increased possibility of the boat's low voltage power supply lines acting as an antenna. In

this way, large voltages may appear on otherwise isolated parts of the electrical system and so cause damage to other electrical equipment aboard.

During a storm it is preferable that the antenna and power supply lines be disconnected from all radio equipment and that the antennas be connected to earth. However, there is a risk attached to handling antennas once a storm has actually started and discharge of static electricity could be achieved by including the arrangement shown in Fig 6.6.

HF transceiver installation

The performance of an HF transceiver is perhaps more influenced by its installation than any other item of boat radio equipment. Its location and the way in which it is set up can account for all the difference between straining to make out some weak station and being able to hold a comfortable conversation.

Perhaps the most critical part of any transceiver installation is the antenna. So much so that the whole of the next chapter is devoted to the subject, but here we look at some important points in planning an installation.

Siting

In choosing a site for an HF transceiver, apart from the obvious need to find somewhere from which it can be operated conveniently, the site must also provide adequate ventilation and thorough protection from splashes of salt water. Even modern transceivers dissipate a fair amount of heat, especially when transmitting at full power.

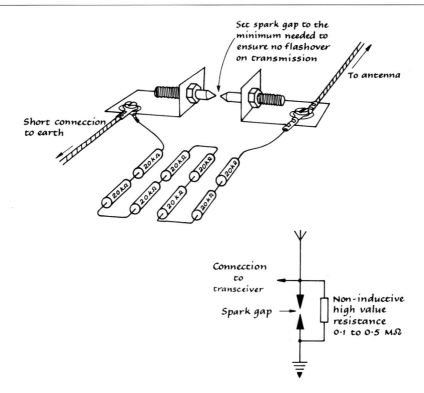

Fig 6.6 High voltage leakage and spark discharge path for antennas.

Older valve sets generate even more and, in either case, if it is not allowed to escape freely, the temperature rise is certain to damage internal components. Many sets are fitted with fans to assist internal cooling and in choosing a site it is vital to ensure that air can circulate freely around all parts of the unit.

Power supply connections

Many transceivers are particularly sensitive to power supply voltage variations (see the section on voltage compatibility, page 83). Transmitting from a low voltage supply can result in a distorted, unintelligible signal, sometimes referred to on SSB as 'FM-ing'. The problem is made worse if the power supply cables are too thin and/or too long as the high

currents drawn on SSB speech peaks lead to large voltage losses.

Cable sizes of 6 or 10sqmm cables are typical but the actual size must depend upon the length and be selected to keep the transceiver operating voltage within the manufacturer's range even when transmitting at full power.

RF grounding

In this context the term grounding refers to the provision of a path for RF current to earth, which in the case of small boats usually means the surrounding sea. The term is not to be confused with the practice of joining the negative connection of batteries, starter motors, alternators, etc to the engine block.

With most installations, the quality of the RF grounding has a significant influence upon overall performance and it is well worth taking pains to ensure that it is effective. On metal boats the ideal RF ground is the hull itself but in the case of wooden or plastic hulls, the solution may be less obvious. What is required is a large area of metal – at least 1sqm, in close proximity to the water. Perhaps surprisingly, physical contact is not essential. In the case of fibre glass hulls one answer is to use a sheet of copper laid against the inside of the hull below the waterline. Its effect is to form a capacitive connection through the hull, through which RF current is able to pass, though of course any DC would be blocked. On new glassfibre hulls quite a neat result can be achieved by bonding a sheet of perforated copper foil beneath the last layer of mat, but few builders are able to achieve such foresight at such an early stage of construction. Other possible means of achieving an effective RF ground include:

• Connection to an external metal keel or at least 1sqm metal (usually copper) attached to the outside of the hull. A metal rudder may also provide sufficient area but do not be tempted to rely upon the propeller, skin fittings and stern gear.
• Connection to an encapsulated solid metal keel. In these cases connection to the sea water is capacitive and again it is important to have sufficient area of metal in close proximity to the water. For this reason, ballast keels that consist of separate blocks of metal are unsuitable and this also includes keels filled with shot or steel punchings.
• Proprietary brands of earthing plates (eg Dynaplate) bolted to the outside of the hull. These proprietary earthing plates are usually constructed from a fused mass of tiny metallic spheres. With this kind of construction, the area of metal in contact with the water is far in excess of that which might be estimated from the overall dimensions of the plate. Smaller models carry the equivalent of 1sqm copper, and larger types intended for lightning protection are also available.

To work effectively it is important that they maintain a good contact with the water. To do this they should not be painted with antifoul. Regular cleaning on haul outs also helps, and here some users have reported that vinegar or other mild acids are effective in removing the scaling that sometimes occurs.

Connection between RF ground and transceiver

As was mentioned at the beginning of this section, the object of the RF ground is to provide a low electrical impedance connection to the sea. This is made up partly by the impedance between the grounding plate (keel or whatever) and the sea, and partly by the impedance of the connection between the plate and the transceiver. To achieve best results the route used for this connection should be as direct as possible and made of low RF impedance material. The traditional material is 25mm x 1mm copper strip, which is a better choice than conventional multistranded cable.

Chapter 7 • Marine antennas

All radio equipment needs some kind of antenna to receive information or send it to the outside world. With some GPS sets or broadcast receivers, it may be hidden entirely inside the case but these perform poorly in metal or steel reinforced concrete boats and external types are usually a great improvement.

Antennas come in bewildering range of shapes and sizes, from the short stub used on some cell phones to long wires for MF transceivers to more complex structures sometimes enclosed in plastic tubes, mushrooms or domes. Size and design is to a large extent dependent on their operating frequency and purpose but they are a critical part of any radio equipment, which makes it well worth learning something about how they work and can be made to perform at their best. In some cases, it's even possible to make your own from parts you may already have on board; a valuable skill that could restore communications in an emergency.

Basic ideas

When dealing for the first time with radio frequency currents and voltages, many people who feel confident in handling most domestic and boat wiring jobs are surprised to find that some firmly held electrical principles no longer seem quite the same. Put a few turns into a cable carrying RF current and the flow is blocked and yet the same current is able to flow into a wire antenna that's not tangibly connected to anything at all; but perhaps these occurrences are not so unusual. Think of interference as a radio signal. In the last chapter we saw how it could be generated by unconnected equipment such as outboards or alternators, and when present on power supply cables, could be blocked by inserting a coil or choke.

Consider the circuits shown in Fig 7.1a to 7.1d, which are all open circuits fed by a power supply of increasing frequency. Fig 7.1a shows the basic case of a wire with one end connected to a DC supply whilst the other remains disconnected and suspended freely. At the moment the switch is closed, current is able to flow into the wire. However, as the wire becomes charged, the flow soon stops and, like any other open circuit, it behaves as a high resistance with no net flow of current either into or out of the wire.

If the DC supply is replaced with an AC, as in Fig 7.1b, provided that the frequency is low and the wire quite short, the arrangement again behaves like a very high resistance. As the polarity of the supply goes positive, current flows in a direction that makes the wire also become positive. Later, as the supply goes negative, so the current flows in the opposite direction and the wire takes on a

a)

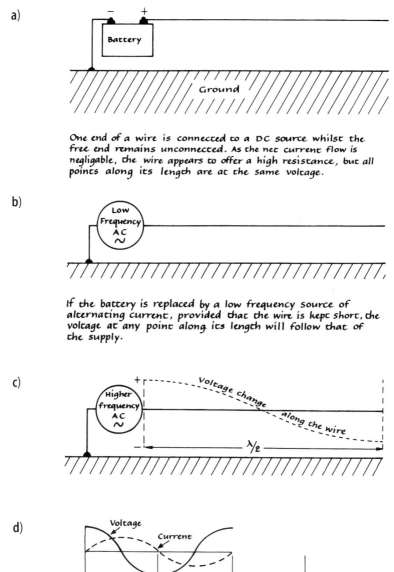

One end of a wire is connected to a DC source whilst the free end remains unconnected. As the net current flow is negligable, the wire appears to offer a high resistance, but all points along its length are at the same voltage.

b)

If the battery is replaced by a low frequency source of alternating current, provided that the wire is kept short, the voltage at any point along its length will follow that of the supply.

c)

d)

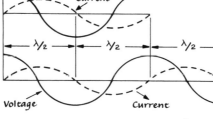

Fig 7.1
a) A DC supply connected to an open wire.
b) A low frequency AC supply connected to an open wire.
c) A high frequency AC supply connected to an open wire.
d) Harmonic resonance on wires of half wavelength multiples.

negative charge. Current in wires travels at speeds close to that of light, so fast that the charge even at the end of the wire appears to follow the polarity of the supply exactly. In this case, although current may be flowing back and forth as the supply changes direction, there is no net flow of current into or out of the wire so, as in Fig 7.1a, the overall resistance is again high.

If the length of the wire or the supply frequency is increased this simple situation changes and the effects become more interesting. As these changes are made, the point is reached when even the speed of light is not enough to allow the voltage on all parts of the wire to follow exactly that of the supply. In these cases, voltage and current distributions vary along the length of the wire. In Fig 7.1c we see the voltage distribution in the special case, where the length of the wire equals half the wave-length λ.

Under this condition, known as *resonance*, a standing wave pattern of voltage and current is set up along the length of the wire. The resistance, or impedance, that the antenna presents to the supply current (ie the radiation resistance) is now reduced and radio frequency energy is radiated into space. If small changes are made to the supply frequency or length of wire, the resonant state is lost, and the antenna resistance increases. However, if larger changes are made such that the length of wire becomes equal to a whole wavelength (or some other whole number multiple of a half wavelength) then resonance is re-established and the antenna resistance falls. Standing wave patterns for some of these cases are shown in Fig 7.1d.

Radiation distribution around a half wave antenna

Most of the radiation from a half wave wire antenna is produced in all directions at right angles to its length; very little is transmitted along its axis. This is illustrated in Fig 7.2, which shows a single large radiation 'lobe' surrounding the wire. At higher harmonics, this pattern becomes more complex as extra lobes are formed, though the antenna is still generally less effective along its axis than it is at right angles. When this type of antenna is connected to a receiver, stations situated in the direction of the lobes can be expected to be received more strongly than those along its length.

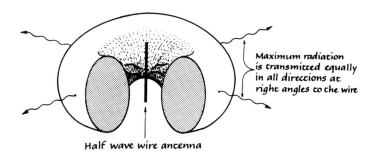

Maximum radiation is transmitted equally in all directions at right angles to the wire

Half wave wire antenna

Fig 7.2 Radiation lobes around a half wave antenna.

Practical MF/HF antennas

When compared with the size of a typical, small ocean sailing or power boat, an ideal antenna for these frequencies is quite long. The problem is worse on MF where, at 2182kHz the length is over 60m (see Table 7.1), so clearly some compromises have to be made to use these bands effectively. Boats also vary greatly in construction, deck and equipment arrangements, type of rig, etc so that it is impossible to arrive at a single design that will give optimum results in all situations. Above all, the antenna must not interfere with normal handling of ropes, rigging or sails and should be as far as possible from the influences of close or overshadowing metallic structures. In fact, the electrical environment in which an antenna is placed can have a profound affect upon its performance and choosing a suitable site invariably requires care, imagination and a few compromises. As a result it is seldom possible to achieve in practice the perfect 'doughnut' shaped radiation patterns described in the last section. This may be distorted in such a way that, in certain directions, radiation is increased yet in others it is reduced. These and other uncertainties make small boat antennas a rather inexact science. With a little thought, it is usually possible to produce a reasonable antenna, though a little experimental work is certain to improve the results. In the section that follows, we look at some simple antenna arrangements from which it should be possible to find at least one that can be adapted to give reasonable results in most situations.

Connection between the transceiver and antenna

The cable connecting a transmitter to its antenna is known as the *feeder*. It may consist of a spaced pair of wires held apart by a plastic separator (ie a balanced feeder), but the use of coaxial (coax) cable is more common. This consists of a central copper conductor surrounded by a plastic insulating material which itself is enclosed within a circular braided copper sheath and covered with a protective plastic outer.

Coax is manufactured in many different grades, but an important property used to distinguish between types is its 'characteristic impedance', which depends upon the size and spacing of the conductors and the nature of the material that separates them. Fifty ohm is the type used for the majority of marine MF, HF and VHF applications and most transceivers are designed to match this impedance. Seventy-five ohm coax is occasionally used for particular types of antennas. The table on page 166 lists some properties of common types of 50 and 75 ohm coax from which it can be seen that, as the working frequency increases, so do the attenuation losses. Those cables with larger overall diameters are usually described as 'low loss' types and are correspondingly more expensive, but their main benefits are of more significance with VHF and higher frequencies rather than HF frequencies.

Coaxial feeders are destroyed by dampness that may creep through the cut ends, or any damaged parts of the outer sheath. Often this is a cause of poor performance in old installations, and on slicing away the outer sheath it's not uncommon to find blue/green copper corrosion products throughout its entire length. When storing coax, make sure that the ends are kept sealed and when installing feeders, take great care to ensure that all connectors are well sealed and that the cable is well protected against mechanical damage.

The half wave dipole

This is one of the most popular and effective types of antenna and is made by splitting the half wave wire of Fig 7.1c into two quarter wave sections. In its simplest form it is essentially a single frequency antenna but, none the less, in practice, it can be effective over a small band of frequencies on either side of its resonant frequency. In addition, it can also work well on others that are harmonically related, though in these cases, technically, it's no longer considered to be a 'half' wave dipole. For example, a dipole cut for 14.175MHz may still be effective on most other frequencies within the 20 metre amateur band as well as some in the 10 metre band. Fig 7.3 shows the constructional details of a dipole antenna, but in practice the actual lengths of each quarter wave leg (L) need to be cut slightly shorter than the theoretical length. For most purposes the practical length for a half wave dipole can be calculated as follows :

1 Take half the theoretical wavelength
  = ½ × (300/frequency in MHz)
2 Reduce this amount by 2.9% (velocity factor)

Frequency (MHz)	Total length of half wave dipole (metres)#
1.8	80.92
*2.182	66.75
4.2	34.68
3.6	40.46
6.4	22.76
7.05	20.67
8.5	17.13
12.7	11.47
14.17	10.28
16.8	8.67
21.2	6.87
22.4	6.50
28.2	5.165
*156.8	0.929

* International distress frequencies.
# Note that the length of each leg will be half this amount.

Table 7.1 Practical lengths for half wave dipoles.

The type of antenna illustrated in Fig 7.3 can give excellent results in spite of having a number of theoretical imperfections. For example, its impedance is 73 ohms, which is a poor match with 50 ohm coax and most transceivers. Half wave dipoles can be quick to make and the materials are usually cheap. This makes them ideal for use in an emergency and gives a possible way of restoring communications following the loss of a main antenna, perhaps through dismasting. In these circumstances, any wire that comes to hand could be pressed into service as long as it can be insulated and has sufficient strength to withstand hoisting. At lower HF and MF, their size may be difficult to accommodate but by cutting for a higher harmonic a working solution may be achieved.

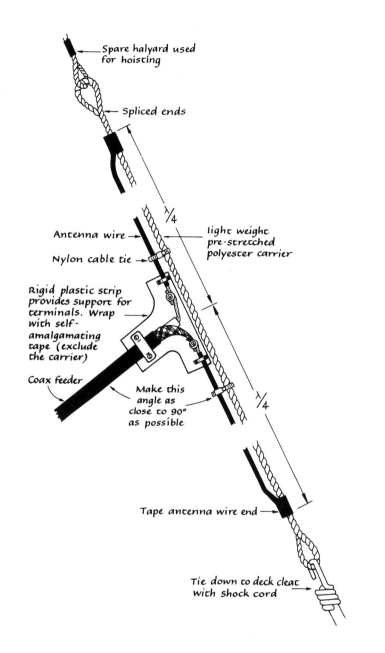

Fig 7.3 Half wave dipole construction details

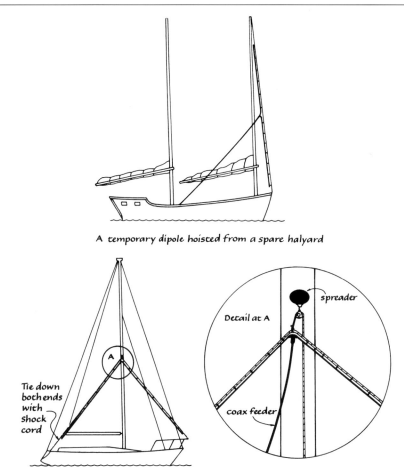

A temporary dipole hoisted from a spare halyard

Tie down both ends with shock cord

Detail at A

spreader

coax feeder

With dipoles that are too long to hoist from the mast head, satisfaction may be obtained by hoisting the centre and tying the ends down. Make the apex angle as large as possible (greater than 90°).

Fig 7.4 Some possible arrangements for hoisting a temporary half wave dipole.

Whip antennas

On very small craft and power boats there may be no rigging suitable for supporting a long wire HF antenna. In these circumstances a whip antenna may provide the best solution but when compared with their VHF equivalent, HF whips are often very much larger. At, say, 150MHz (the mid VHF) the length of a half wave is 1m, whereas at 15MHz (the mid HF), it is ten times greater. Any whip built to these proportions would indeed be enormous and a correspondingly substantial support structure would be required to hold it in place. For these reasons, commercially made HF whips are usually considerably shorter and include somewhere along their length a 'loading coil' that makes up the difference between the physical length and the required electrical length.

Whip antennas manufactured for amateur markets should be inspected very carefully if they are to be permanently

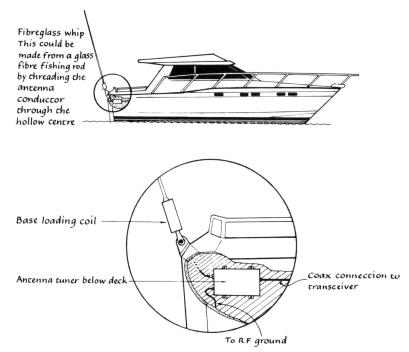

Fig 7.5 A whip antenna aboard a powerboat.

installed aboard a boat. Some manufacturers make only feeble attempts at waterproofing, or use materials that quickly corrode in a marine environment (eg chromium plated steel or zinc/aluminium alloys). Beware, also, of those that contain heavy loading coils near the middle or top of the whip as these may impose unfair loading on the mounting structures as they swing about in a seaway.

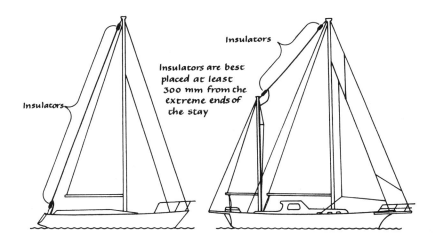

Fig 7.6 Backstay and triatic antennas.

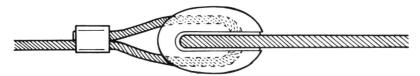

Pyrex or porcelain 'egg' insulators are traditional but will not withstand high rigging loads.

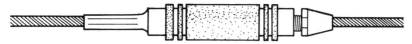

Plastic rigging insulators are available with a variety of end terminals. These include spade and eye fittings, swage and Norse or Stalock swageless terminals and can carry the full working load of the wire.

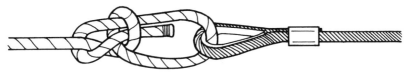

Polyester rope acts as a good insulator

Fig 7.7 Antenna insulator details

Random wire antennas

On many boats, a satisfactory antenna can be made from an existing section of wire rigging. Such a wire can be fed from coax cable connected at one end, and to isolate it from other parts of the boat's rig, insulators will be required at both ends.

Any stay chosen to act as an antenna should not run close to other parts of the boat's metalwork and should have at least 8m (26ft) of length between the insulators. If it is shorter than this, tuning the lower frequency bands may be difficult, though performance in the middle and upper HF range could be satisfactory.

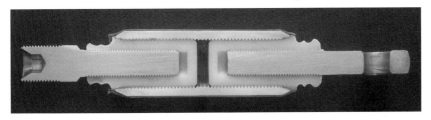

Fig 7.8 Internal section of a Norse rigging insulator, where loads are transmitted through threaded plastic and brass or bronze outer sleeve. After ten years of service the white plastic insulating material was crumbling where exposed, possibly due to UV exposure, and showing clear signs of decay. The manufacturers advise inspection and replacement on a regular basis.

A major attraction of rigging antennas is that they are unlikely to interfere with the normal working of the boat, but since rigging was not primarily intended for this purpose it's quite likely that the length will not be related to any particular frequency that you might wish to use. If it is possible to arrange the insulators so that the antenna length is equal to a half wavelength at a working frequency (including the length of the feeder), then so much the better. In other cases, and if you want to use the antenna on a range of bands that are not harmonically related, an antenna tuning unit will be needed. This is a device that uses combinations of inductors and capacitors to effectively alter the electrical length of the antenna, thus enabling it to tune a range of frequencies.

Antenna matchers/tuners

These are used to match the impedance of a random length of wire or other non-resonant antenna to the 50 ohm impedance required by transceivers. If this is not done, power to the antenna is not transferred efficiently and damage to the transmitter output stage may result. There are several proprietary types on the market, with several claiming to provide a 50 ohm impedance from any length of antenna. This may be so, but it does not mean that they are able to make any length of wire into an effective radiator at any frequency. Inevitably, best results are obtained only at frequencies at which the antenna is able to resonate. Antenna tuners fall broadly into two types – manual and automatic.

Manual tuners

These include a meter to measure power transferred to the antenna and a set of controls that need to be reset each time the transceiver frequency is changed. The MFJ model shown in Fig 7.9 is a typical example and frequently used aboard small boats.

Because of the need for routine adjustment, for convenience, manual tuners are usually sited close to the transceiver. In these cases a fairly long run of coax is often needed to connect to the antenna itself, but as far as the tuner is concerned, this cable is also

Fig 7.9 The MFJ-949E manual antenna tuner (courtesy MFJ Enterprises).

part of the antenna. If coax is used, it is unable to function as such and if coax is not used, there is the possibility that radiated RF energy will cause feedback difficulties with other equipment on board. Some makes of autopilot are particularly sensitive; the problem becoming obvious when the boat changes course as someone speaks on the radio.

Building your own manual tuner is a job that's well within the capabilities of most home constructors and many designs have been published in the amateur radio literature. Kits are also available but, in choosing any type of tuner, check to see that it is designed at least to handle the maximum power of your transceiver and that it is solidly constructed from good quality components.

Automatic tuners

If you seldom switch frequencies, manual tuners are fine but otherwise the continual need to readjust their settings can become a chore. Automatic tuners overcome this

Fig 7.10 Barrett 911 automatic antenna tuner (courtesy of Barrett Communications).

	Advantages	**Disadvantages**
Manual	• Rugged • Little to go wrong • Needs no power supply • Low cost	• Requires manual readjustment when the frequency is changed • Has to be mounted in a position where manual adjustment is possible
Automatic	• Convenience – no working adjustments needed • With no need for routine adjustment can be mounted in the optimum position, close to the antenna	• Complex and relatively delicate • Repairs can often only be carried out by manufacturer-trained specialists • High cost

Table 7.2 Summary of manual and automatic tuner benefits.

difficulty through the use of sensing circuits to measure transferred power and which are connected to controls to readjust the tuner settings accordingly. With no need for routine adjustment, the cable connecting it to the antenna can be kept short by mounting the unit as close as possible to the antenna. Siting it within a protective enclosure or bolted to the deck or stern rail is a common option and, if this is not possible, consider mounting it immediately below deck (Fig 7.5) or perhaps within a locker.

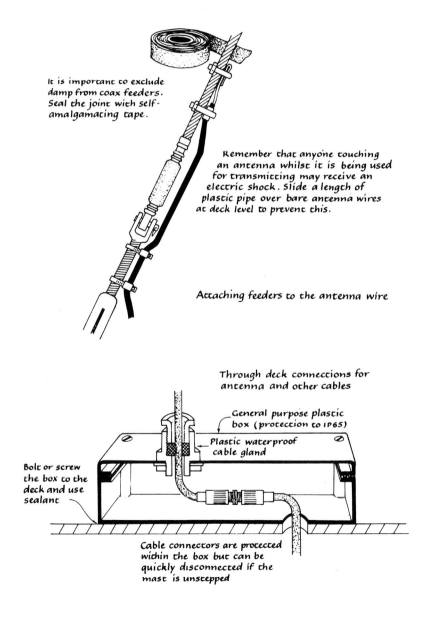

It is important to exclude damp from coax feeders. Seal the joint with self-amalgamating tape.

Remember that anyone touching an antenna whilst it is being used for transmitting may receive an electric shock. Slide a length of plastic pipe over bare antenna wires at deck level to prevent this.

Attaching feeders to the antenna wire

Through deck connections for antenna and other cables

General purpose plastic box (protection to IP65)

Plastic waterproof cable gland

Bolt or screw the box to the deck and use sealant

Cable connectors are protected within the box but can be quickly disconnected if the mast is unstepped

Fig 7.11 Antenna feeder and deck seal details.

Antenna testing

Maximum power can only be transferred to an antenna system when its impedance is equal to (ie matched to) the impedance of the transmitter output. If the match is poor, the antenna will only radiate part of the power supplied, while the remainder is reflected back to the transmitter, causing possible damage to its RF output stage. For this reason, before transmitting on a new antenna system or after making adjustments, it is most important to check that matching is correct.

Standing Wave Ratio (SWR) meters

These are used to measure the ratio of forward to reflected power in antenna feed lines and provide useful confirmation that your antenna and tuner are performing correctly. On better quality amateur transceivers and in some tuners, these are a built-in feature, or they can be bought as a stand alone unit to be coupled into the feeder when checks are needed.

With a perfectly matched antenna the SWR will be 1:1 though this is seldom achieved in practice, so a close minimum value is usually accepted. Ratios of 2:1 or even 3:1 are not too serious but definite action should be taken on values of 3.5:1 or greater. This is the value at which the protective circuits on most modern transceivers begin to operate by reducing power to avoid damage.

SWR meters are often combined with a power meter and include a switch for changing between the two functions. Some transceivers have them conveniently built into the front panel. They are sometimes included on tuners as well but they are ideally connected close to the transmitter.

When tuning an antenna, **use only low power** and, above all, follow the golden rule of before transmitting on any frequency, always **listen first and make sure that it's not already in use**.

Use of a dummy load

Sometimes it is necessary to test a transmitter under load, but it would be wrong to do this while it is connected to an antenna as the interference could well cause difficulties for other radio users. The answer lies in the use of a dummy load, which is a high wattage (often oil cooled), low inductive resistor that can be

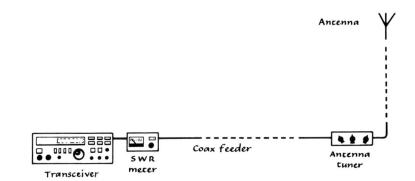

Fig 7.12 Connections between a transceiver, SWR meter, tuner and antenna. The SWR meter checks the current/voltage ratio along the feedline.

connected instead of the antenna. Its resistance (usually 50 ohms) is designed to match the transmitter output, and metal screening ensures that no RF signal is radiated.

Practical VHF antennas

Almost without exception, marine VHF antennas are whips. Frequency dictates that they are physically much smaller than their MF/HF equivalents, making them less intrusive and easier to accommodate. Because

propagation on VHF is essentially 'line of sight' (see Table 1.2), their ideal mounting spot is on the highest part of the boat, usually the masthead.

Because all marine VHF frequencies are in the same band and relatively close together, no separate tuner is used and the antenna plugs directly into the transceiver. When purchasing, sound mechanical construction, durability of components and waterproofing are major considerations.

Another factor to consider is the antenna gain. In this context, the term gain does not

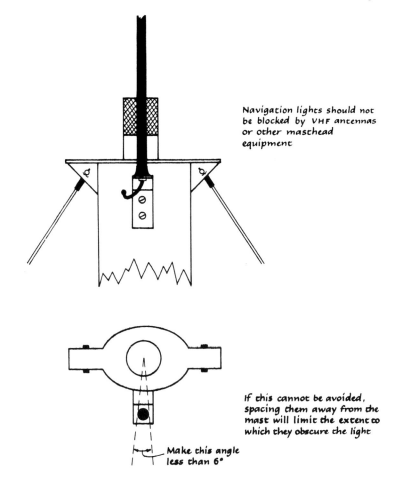

Navigation lights should not be blocked by VHF antennas or other masthead equipment

If this cannot be avoided, spacing them away from the mast will limit the extent to which they obscure the light

Make this angle less than 6°

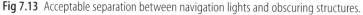

Fig 7.13 Acceptable separation between navigation lights and obscuring structures.

Fig 7.14 Radiation patterns around high and low gain whip antennas.

mean amplification but compares the signal emitted in a horizontal direction to that of a theoretically perfect omnidirectional antenna. High gain antennas are designed to focus more signal in a horizontal direction and are a sensible choice for non-heeling craft such as power vessels or perhaps multihulls. On a monohull sailing boat, a signal received on the same antenna would be likely to fade in and out as the vessel heels so, instead, a more omni-directional, ie lower gain antenna, is more appropriate.

Higher gain antennas are also longer and require more substantial mountings, which are more easily achieved on the deck of a power boat rather than the masthead of a yacht.

Gain	Typical overall length (m)
3db	1.2
6db	2.5
9db	7.0

Table 7.3 Typical overall lengths of VHF antennas of various gains.

Receiver antennas

Design principles for receiver antennas follow similar lines to those for transmitters. An antenna designed to transmit on a particular frequency will also be good for receiving the same, but the converse is not always true. In general, receivers are far less demanding of their antenna systems and bad matching will not cause damage, though the received signal strength may be greatly reduced.

Short wave and broadcast receivers are usually fitted with an internal ferrite rod antenna for reception on medium and long wave broadcasts. Most also have a telescopic antenna for VHF, FM and short wave reception but, with either type, reception of anything other than strong local stations is likely to be improved with an external antenna, even if it's just a random length of light wire hoisted on a spare halyard or tied between rigging wires. This is particularly true if you have a metal or ferro cement boat, in which case reception on portable radios below deck may be impossible due the screening effect of the hull. Interference caused by noisy on-board electrical equipment can exacerbate the difficulties but by being further away from the source, an external antenna may again provide the solution.

Active antennas

Active antennas are suitable for receivers only but their name is somewhat misleading as it describes not an antenna, but an extremely wide band RF amplifier that is used to increase the signal from a conventional antenna.

The strongest signals produced by an antenna will normally be on the frequency at which it resonates. However, a broad spectrum of other frequencies will also be present and the job of a radio receiver is to ignore all except the particular frequency we wish to listen to. Particularly with short antennas, lower frequency signals may be very weak, and an 'active' amplifier can significantly improve the reception.

Active antennas are quite small devices, generally fitted close to the antenna rather than the receiver. Some fit easily into a matchbox and although a power supply is required current drain is usually very low. There are several types on the market, some in kit form and simple enough for most people to assemble within a few hours.

Some advertisers promote them as a universal panacea for bad reception but this is not always the case. Problems can stem from the fact that, because they are wide band amplifiers, they amplify all signals – the strong along with the weak. On the receiver the effect is that although the wanted signals are amplified, so too are all background noises and interference. Furthermore, if strong signals are present, even at some distance from the required frequency, they can overload its RF section, causing them to break in on the wanted frequency. The solution lies in providing RF tuning or filtering of the signal before it reaches the receiver, and the inclusion of a small antenna tuner would do much to alleviate the problem. It would of course need re-tuning as the frequency is changed, but since it would not be used for transmitting, it could be quite lightly constructed.

Chapter 8 • **Computer modes**

Spend a few idle moments scanning through frequencies on the HF bands and many of the transmissions that you hear will be in code. To an untrained ear they are easily mistaken for interference rather than any kind of sensible broadcast, but given the means to unscramble them you can discover a wealth of information, including fax pictures, weather reports, agency news, navigational data, e-mail and clandestine broadcasters.

Different services encode their transmissions in different ways. Slow scan television has a warbling sound, Weatherfax is like someone stroking a brick with coarse sandpaper, packet radio is an interrupted series of brruuuuuuuups and Navtex rather like a few loose stones in a car hubcap. All are difficult to convey in words, but obvious when you've learnt to identify them.

Decoding data transmissions

In the past, the only way of working with data transmissions was to buy a separate piece of equipment for each mode, eg a Navtex machine for Navtex, a telex machine for telex, a Weatherfax machine for Weatherfax, etc. On vessels with sufficient space and power to accommodate the equipment this approach does have certain advantages:

• Failure of one item does not affect the others.
• Operating procedures can be kept simple.

These days, the alternative approach is to use a computer and suitable software. All that's needed for some data modes, apart from cables to interconnect between the microphone and speakers on the radio and computer, is a sound card. For others, the job is best carried out by a small dedicated computer with digital signal processing abilities. These are variously known as data decoders, TNCs (Terminal Node Controllers) or simply as modems and have no screen or keyboard (see Figs 8.4 & 8.5). Rather like the telephone modem that connects between a computer and phone line, these devices connect between the computer and radio. We'll look at them in more detail later in the chapter.

Radio requirements

Most better quality receivers (or transceivers) can be used for receiving data transmissions, but they should be capable of being tuned to within 1kHz. Within 0.1kHz would be better and the ideal would be one tenth of this. Once set to a particular frequency, it is important that it does not drift as this will make tuning of some transmissions frustrating, if not impossible (drift is dependent upon

Where to listen for data transmissions

Several internet sites carry sound clip samples of various data transmissions and are a useful beginners' guide to identification (see www.pangolin.co.nz/radio/).

Real examples, sometimes mixed with interference, can be found in all parts of the radio spectrum. The following table provides a list of some of the more likely spots, but increase your chances of finding them by listening on and around the following frequencies.

Mode	Frequency (MHz)
Morse (USB)	14.00, 14.200
	21.00 - 21.150
	27.450, 27.680
SSTV (USB)	27.600
	21.340, 21.320, 21.350
	14.230, 14.239, 14.260
Navtex	0.518
AMTOR (LSB)	14.040 – 14.110
	21.000 – 21.150
	27.600
Pactor (LSB)	14.040 - 14.110
	21.00 - 21.150
PSK31	3.580, 3.610
	10.140
	14.070
	28.120
SSTV (USB)	27.600
	21.340, 21.320, 21.350
	14.230, 14.239, 14.260

temperature but should be less than 50Hz/hour).

If you are transmitting data, a point to keep in mind is that the transmitter is working harder than when sending SSB speech, and as a result more current is drawn from the power supply. Pay particular attention to antenna/transceiver impedance matching to avoid transceiver damage, and to power supply cable thickness to ensure that full voltage is available even at peak loads.

With ARQ TOR codes and related codes (covered later), the transceiver is required to switch rapidly between transmit and receive.

With AMTOR the transition in either direction (ie transmit to receive or receive to transmit) must be accomplished in less than 50ms, but with commercial full duplex versions of the code the frequency is switched at the same time. Most modern transceivers are able to cope but some older models are not. Delay in the receive/transmit switching time sets a theoretical limit on the maximum distance over which communications may be carried out.

Computer requirements

When choosing a computer for use at sea, the smaller size, lower power consumption and compact size of Notebooks are obvious plus points. Most models come with a charger to plug into the mains although a more efficient option would be to run it from the boat's batteries. For some makes, adaptors that plug into a car cigarette lighter socket are available as an extra and are a more efficient power source.

Aboard larger boats, where mains power is easily available, a standard office desktop machine is worth considering. Costs are lower and repairs, upgrading and maintenance easier. In a dry boat, there is no reason why life expectancy should be any less than in a similar dry environment ashore. From my own experience, over some 20 years, I've never lost an item of domestic grade electrical equipment through marine corrosion. However, this time has been spent mainly spent in latitudes of less than 35° with the boat in continuous use. For boats in colder climates that are left sealed and unattended for long periods, complete removal and dry shoreside storage of all electronics would be a wise precaution.

Typically, 50 per cent of the power used by desktop computers with CRT (Cathode Ray Tube) monitors is taken by the display. Use of

Computer safety

1 Make absolutely sure that the computer and all its accessories and wiring are well secured and protected. This applies to Notebook and office machines alike and can't be overemphasised. The standard of installation that is the norm ashore has no place at sea.

2 If you are using mains power, ensure that the installation is to marine standards. Use a solid state flat screen monitor in preference to a CRT.

Most standard CRT monitors have a case that is perforated with many holes as an aid to cooling. As well as allowing air to circulate they can easily also allow water to enter and wash over the tube and power supply, which produces an output of several thousand volts.

In an accident that occurred in late 2001 in Queensland, Australia, a crew member was passing time during some heavy weather by playing a computer game in the wheelhouse. A wave crashed against a window, smashing it in and flooding over both the computer and crew member, who was killed by electrocution.

a solid state flat screen monitor can bring substantial energy savings and since most run on low voltages, there is also a safety advantage.

Irrespective of the relative merits of different types of computers and operating systems, most radio software is written for the PC running Microsoft Windows. Use anything else and you may find your choice of software more limited and some applications simply not available. However, if you are using an external hardware data decoder, demands on the computer are not great and a 486 machine running Windows 95 or later could be sufficient. If you are using a software decoder for Navtex, Weatherfax, etc, a sound card with speakers and microphone socket will probably be required.

Software decoders

There are several software titles on the market; some available from the larger marine stores, some that can be downloaded from the web and some that are shareware (see www.pangolin.co.nz/radio for current listings).

Early types used an interface connection between the radio's phone or extension speaker jack and the computer's serial (ie com or RS232) port. The connecting lead included a small amount of electronics to convert the radio's audio into a signal that could be handled by the serial port. These programs are still available but for computers with sound cards, those that use the card's line input and output sockets (or microphone and speaker) are a better option because they are purpose built to handle audio whereas the serial port is not. In this case, the only extra hardware

that's required is a length of coax with suitable plugs to connect between the sound card's microphone input and the radio's audio output.

Written by Eberhard Backeshoff (DK8JV), Jvcomm32 is a typical example from this group. It's a shareware program that can be downloaded from the web in a free trial form. If you like the program and intend to continue using it you are expected to pay a modest registration fee. Fig 8.1 shows a screen shot of it in action receiving a Weatherfax image.

Jvcomm 32 is a particularly versatile program and in addition to Weatherfax it can also be used to receive and display slow scan television pictures and images from polar orbiting and geostationary weather satellites. Other sound card decoders have the ability to decode Navtex, AMTOR, and Pactor. We'll look at these modes in more detail later.

Weatherfax

HF Weatherfax is a good point from which to start learning about data modes. For more information on reception and interpretation of weatherfax and satellite images see *Understanding Weatherfax*, Mike Harris (Adlard Coles 2002). This is a service that has been in existence for many decades and although some countries have made moves to phase it out in favour of 'user pay' schemes, it is a robust system and highly valued by small craft users.

A typical chart, such as that in Fig 8.1, takes around eight to 20 minutes to receive. These are broadcast by stations around the world at scheduled times of the day so, to receive a particular type of weather chart, you'll need to know which frequencies to listen on and at what times to listen. This information is

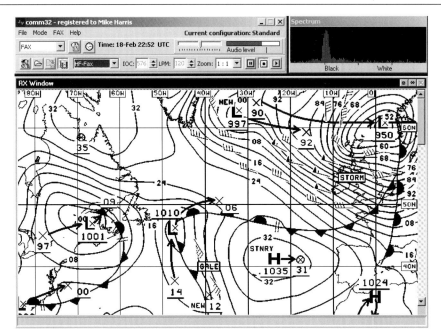

Fig 8.1 JVcomm32 receiving an HF Weatherfax surface analysis.

provided in the station's schedule, which changes from time to time but is usually published on the internet.

Weatherfax transmissions are formed by switching between a pair of tones used to denote black and white and consist of the following audibly distinctive parts:

Start tone This is formed by fast (300Hz) switching between black and white tones and is used as a start signal for automated receivers.

Phasing signal or sync pulse A repeated blip appearing as a rectangular block on the screen and used to mark the top left corner of the image.

Test scale or tone bar Not all stations use this but when present it is heard as a whistle of sliding frequency. On a correctly tuned radio and computer, it appears as a band that progressively changes from black to white.

Image body This is the longest part of the transmission and carries image data.

Stop tone Sounds like the start tone but switched at a frequency of 450Hz.

Unmodulated carrier Some stations carry on to send a continuous black tone signal for a few moments.

Fax stations often transmit the same chart at different times of the day and on different frequencies so if using HF propagation predictions as a guide, use only those that are expected to give the best results.

Not all program help files are well written so if you are experiencing difficulties and don't find the answers you need, try another program. However, tuning the radio and software settings to achieve really good results is something that comes with practice and familiarity so be prepared for a certain amount of trial and error when starting out.

Polar orbiting weather satellite images

These satellites orbit the Earth at an altitude of 800 to 1000 km (497–621 miles) and, as their name suggests, they travel in orbits that pass close to the Poles. The US NOAA satellites are a typical example and travel in the opposite direction to the Earth's rotation. They execute about 14.2 orbits per day, crossing the equator at an angle of around 98°. These are known as Sun synchronous orbits and pass over the same part of the Earth each day.

They travel in a north–south or south–north direction and their cameras continually scan the Earth below in an east–west direction, thus producing a never-ending picture strip. Their transmissions are in the VHF band and higher frequencies so an observer on the Earth is only able to receive them when the satellite is above his/her local horizon. Times at which a particular satellite will come into view can be calculated in advance with a satellite tracking program. This allows you to plan the times to have your equipment set up and listening and gives an indication of ground area that the image you are about to receive will cover.

The image transmissions of most interest to marine users are termed 'low resolution' and are broadcast in frequency modulated VHF in a format known as APT (Automatic Picture Transmission). They are sent at a rate of 120 lines per minute, giving an effective data rate of 32K bits/second.
Signal strengths are relatively strong, but at around 137MHz the frequency is a little above

Geostationary satellite type	Frequencies (MHz)		
NOAA	137.500	137.620	
Meteor	137.300	137.400	137.85

Table 8.1 Frequencies used by polar orbiting satellites.

FM radio broadcasts and below amateur and marine band VHF.

The required bandwidth of 42MHz is also a little narrower than that used by broadcast radios but wider than that of communications receivers. For good results, a purpose built radio is usually necessary. The antenna, too, is a little unusual and although a simple whip sometimes works, it needs to be of a type that can receive signals from any direction. Fig 8.2 shows a type commonly used aboard boats.

See the links section on page 169 for internet sources giving more details on satellite image reception, equipment software and operating practice. See also www.pangolin.co.nz/weatherfax.html.

Slow scan television

This is a quick and convenient means of sending colour pictures over HF radio. Depending on the versatility of the software you are using, pictures can be sent as bitmap files, JPGs, TIFs or any of the common image formats, with the possible exception of GIFs. A good way to begin is to practise receiving pictures sent by practised users. Since SSTV is mainly an amateur activity they are not difficult to find. Begin by looking around 14.250MHz in the 20 metre band.

SSTV is transmitted in a number of slightly different variants with trade-offs between

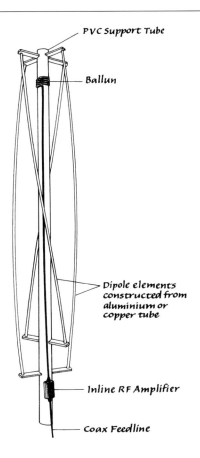

PVC Support Tube

Ballun

Dipole elements
constructed from
aluminium or
copper tube

Inline RF Amplifier

Coax Feedline

Fig 8.2 A quadrifilar antenna for image reception from polar orbiters.

SSTV mode	Duration (seconds)	Size
Robot 36	36	320 x 240
Robot 72	72	320 x 240
AVT 90	90	320 x 240
Scottie 1	110	320 x 256
Scottie 2	71	320 x 256
Scottie DX	269	320 x 256
Martin 1	114	320 x 256
Martin 2	58	320 x 256
SC2-180	182	320 x 256
SC2-120	122	320 x 256
PD 50	50	320 x 256
PD 90	90	320 x 256

Table 8.2 Slow scan television modes.

picture size, transmission time and colour rendition. Table 8.2 lists some of the more common modes.

Popularity of each mode varies between regions with Scottie 1 common in North America and Martin 1 a favourite with Europeans. Amateur operators often say which they are using in a voice transmission before they begin but if you are unclear which is in use inspired trial and error may bring results.

When transmitting picture files, the software converts their binary data into an audio stream. Without the radio connected, you can listen to SSTV signals by sending a file and listening to the audio from your computer's speakers. Some surprisingly good results have been achieved simply by placing the radio's microphone close to the computer (see Fig 8.3a & b), but for a more serious effort a cable connection would be a distinct improvement.

Navtex

Sound card software is also available for decoding Navtex broadcasts, but when compared with a dedicated receiver lacks the convenience of being able to standby for long periods on reduced power.

The code used is derived from early telex but adapted for use over radio to include a method of error checking that allows the receiving station to check received characters. Codes used for transmission of text have changed enormously over the years and those now in use for e-mail and data are far faster,

Fig 8.3a & 8.3b SSTV images by Tom May aboard *Optimum Trust* in the South Pacific as received 4000 miles away by Bob Reed in Humboldt Bay, California (both using Jvcomm32) show what can be done with minimal equipment. Originals were in colour and taken with a digital camera, and transmitted simply by holding the HF transceiver's microphone close to the speaker on the laptop computer.
a) Wharf at Canton Island.   b) Crew member Angela from the UK.

more reliable and use less bandwidth than their predecessors. In the next section, we review some of the major codes that are in current use.

TOR (Telex On Radio) codes

This family of codes was introduced for maritime use several decades ago and was called SITOR (Simplex Telex On Radio). All use FSK (Frequency Shift Keying) to encode binary data, which uses a pair of audio tones to encode. They are typically 200Hz apart and following an old teleprinter tradition they are called 'mark' and 'space' corresponding to binary '1' and '0'.

In the late 1970s the marine code was adapted for amateur use by Peter Martinez (G3PLX) when it became known as AMTOR, though there are more similarities than differences between the systems.

Two versions are in regular use and these are ARQ (Automatic Repeat Request or sometimes simply called mode A) and FEC (Forward Error Correction or mode B). The type used depends upon whether the transmission is intended for reception by a single station, such as a personal telex, or as a broadcast to many stations as would be used for a Navtex transmission.

ARQ

Once you have heard the repetitive chirping sound by stations using this mode, it's hard to mistake it for anything else. The sending station transmits a block of three characters which the receiving station examines for errors. If they appear credible, the receiving station transmits to the sender a control code requesting the next block of three and, if not,

it sends a code asking for them to be repeated. In this way, both sender and receiver transmit alternately, hence the characteristic ARQ chirp. At times when regular voice communications are blighted by fading, interference or static, the ARQ mode can still be effective. Such conditions may lead to many receiving errors and hence more repeat requests, but error free copy may still be achieved.

Although intended for communications between single stations, do not be misled into believing there is any privacy in this mode. Any suitably equipped station can listen in on transmissions and although they'll not be able to make repeat requests, the results may be easily intelligible.

FEC

FEC makes a jangling, stone in a hubcap type of sound. Because it's intended for reception by many stations, individual receiving stations are unable to request repeats, so a different method of error correction is necessary. In FEC, each character sent is repeated five characters later. In other words, the whole message is sent twice by interleaving a copy of itself that is displaced by five characters.

The transmission is begun with a phasing signal that is repeated at intervals and which tells the receiving station where and when to expect the repeats. If identical, paired characters are not received, a missed character symbol is placed in the text. The system is simple, reasonably good over a noisy radio link and can be used for casual conversations between stations or group discussions as one would do with a voice channel.

Pactor 1

In the late 1980s, a small group of German amateurs began work on a project to improve existing AMTOR protocols. One of the objectives was to improve protocols that had previously been successful on VHF but less effective on HF. The result was Pactor 1, and claimed the following improvements over AMTOR:

• Transmission of a full ASCII character set including upper and lower case letters.
• Transmission speeds set at 100 or 200 bauds depending on band conditions.
• Data compression. Pactor 1 transmits 20 characters per frame compared to AMTOR's three. This allows data compression to be used giving increased speed.

Pactor 1 also offers ARQ and FEC modes and has been widely used for e-mail traffic although it has now largely been replaced by GTor and Pactor 2. In the early 1990s the development team formed the German company SCS (Special Communications Systems GmbH & Co., KG, Roentgenstr. 36, 63454 Hanau, Germany) that now manufacture hardware modems and continue to develop the mode.

GTor

Devised by M Golay in the US, GTor is marketed by Kantronics (Kantronics, 1202 East 23rd Street, Lawrence, Kansas 66046, US) and was first introduced in 1994. Like AMTOR, it has an ARQ mode but instead of three characters per frame, all frames are 19.2 seconds in duration and contain variable amounts of data. The actual number of characters is either 24, 48 or 72, depending on the speed of sending, which

is either 100, 200 or 300 bauds and which in turn depends on band conditions. Claimed improvements over AMTOR were:

• Transmission of a full ASCII character set including upper and lower case letters.
• Variable transmission speeds, depending on band conditions.
• Error detection by 16 bit CRC (Cyclic Redundancy Check).
• Apparent reduction in the effects of interference.
• Substantially higher data rates achieved by Huffman data compression.

Under good conditions, GTor is significantly faster than Pactor 1 and is used by some HF e-mail services. Perhaps because it is only available from a single manufacturer, it has not been adopted as quickly as its advantages might suggest.

Pactor 2

Also developed by SCS, Pactor 2 is radically different from the earlier version. The main changes are two-tone, phase-shift encoding (PSK) and the use of a DSP (Digital Signal Processor) and dedicated 32 bit micro-processor. The result is a more robust code that performs better under weak signal conditions and at an absolute maximum speed of 800bps though with compression, received rates can increase by 1.5 to 1.9 times.

The main drawback of Pactor 2 is that the more complex signal processing has led to increased costs. It is unlikely that anyone will perfect a Pactor 2 sound card decoder, at least not using the current generation of cards, which means that a dedicated hardware modem is required. Costs are falling but at

Bauds, bits and words

Several terms are used to describe the speed of data transmissions making it difficult to compare one with another unless you know exactly what's meant.

Bauds

Named after the early teleprinter pioneer JME Baudot, they are defined as the number of data line state changes per second.

bps

Binary bits per second or the number of '0s' or '1s' per second. Although technically different, in many cases, this is numerically identical to the baud rate.

wpm

Words per minute. In quantifying data speeds a 'standard' word length of five characters is assumed, although some agencies use 6.1 characters. As a guide, the following table gives an approximate comparison between baud rates and wpm:

Bauds	WPM
45	60
50	67
57	75
75	100
100	132
110	147
150	200
200	267
300	400

In converting between bauds/bps and words remember that, depending on the code, a proportion of the characters sent are control codes and not a printable part of the message text. The use of data compression will also affect the relationship by increasing the number of printable characters.

present expect to pay 45 per cent more for a Pactor 2 modem than for one that doesn't include this mode. In the world of data transmissions, speed is everything and, in spite of the cost, Pactor 2 has become an established standard for HF e-mail.

Pactor 3

A web search for Pactor reveals the existence of at least five Pactor variants. At the time of writing Pactor 3 is the most recent and is quoted as being four to five times faster than its predecessor. Users of old Pactor 2 modems can obtain it as a firmware upgrade at a price that's considerably lower than the cost of a complete new modem.

Other data modes

In this section, it's been possible only to give a brief overview of the data modes of most interest to marine users, but there are plenty more. Some interesting new modes, now being developed mainly by amateurs, include PSK31, MT63, NEWQPSK and the Hellschreiber family. Clearly, not all are destined to replace Pactor, though all do have special individual benefits and their development over the next few years will be worth watching.

Hardware data controllers (HF modems)

These are small, self contained computers, usually with few controls other than some status lights and a tuning indicator. They are connected to a transceiver's microphone and audio output jack and to the computer, usually via the serial data port.

Advantages of using a hardware data controller over sound card software are:

- The computer and signal processing circuits contained within the controller are purpose built for the single task of handling radio data.
- Demands on the main computer hardware are lower; often you can get away with using a machine that's a few years out of date and without a sound card or other 'extras'.

With the exception of SSTV, for modes that involve transmitting as well as receiving data, a hardware controller generally does a neater job. For e-mail it is virtually essential and the choice is between one that supports Pactor 1, which is probably OK if you are a light user and only need to send the odd message once in a while, or to pay the extra cost for the greater speed of a Pactor 2 controller. Actually, the choice is not quite that simple as these units can be used for far more than just e-mail, but we will look at one example of each and the additional features they offer.

The Kantronics KAM XL

The main features of this unit are:

- Modes covered include Pactor 1, GTor, AMTOR, Navtex, RTTY, PSK31, ASCII, WEFAX, Morse and packet radio.
- Easily upgradeable to cover future modes and protocols.

Fig 8.4 The Kantronics KAM XL.

- Complete operating manual can be downloaded from the web.
- Has an NMEA 0183 interface for GPS connection.
- Has dual radio ports and can cover VHF and HF operation.
- Size: 125 x 43 x 183mm.
- Consumes 150 mA at 10 to 18 volts.

The SCS PTC IIe

The main features of this unit are:

- Modes covered include Pactor 1, Pactor 2, AMTOR, Navtex, RTTY, PSK31, SSTV, Weatherfax, Morse and packet radio.
- Has a single transceiver port.
- Complete operating manual can be downloaded from the web.
- Programmable mark and space frequencies.
- Output amplitude is programmable in millivolt steps.
- Can be turned on or off under software control.
- Size: 125 x 43 x 183mm.
- Consumes 200 mA at 13.8 volts.

Installation

The toughest part of learning to use a data controller is understanding the documentation. Because they are multipurpose devices, there is plenty of it and much that you'll not need, but it takes time to separate sections on general operation from those covering details of modes that you may never use.

Unfortunately, there are no standard plug and socket configurations for connecting controllers to computers and radios so be prepared to modify those supplied with the unit. All that can be said is that there are three cables:

1 Power supply to the data controller.
2 Audio input from the transceiver. (Make sure that this does not disable the radio's loudspeaker as it is essential to be able to listen on the band before transmitting).
3 Audio output from the controller to the transceiver, including a connection to the microphone's PTT (Push To Talk) line.

Use screened cable for audio lines and make sure that ground connections are secure.

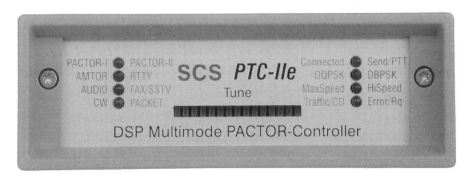

Fig 8.5 Front panel of the SCS PTC IIe showing status lights and tuning indicator.

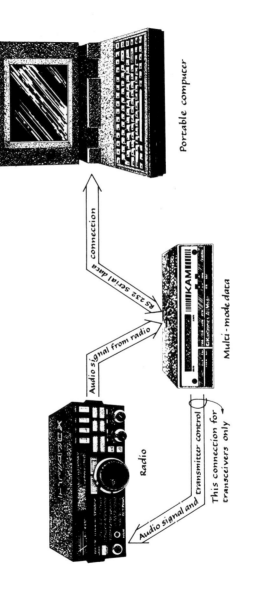

Fig 8.6 Interfacing a data controller to a radio and portable computer.

Software for data controllers

Data controller software is needed to allow the main computer to issue command instructions to the controller and to display data that it has received or is to transmit. Often it's supplied with the controller and, although rudimentary, is sufficient to get you started. Sooner or later you may discover shortcomings and the need for more functionality. An e-mail program, for example, may be more useful if it handles as many of the control functions for you as possible and looks and feels more like regular e-mail software with the ability to run an address book and manage 'In' and 'Out' mail boxes.

With your data controller, transceiver and computer hardware set up and working together, the potentially more troublesome part is behind you and you can concentrate on getting results. In the next chapter, we look more closely at software and services that are now available to you.

Chapter 9 • E-mail and the internet

In the space of only a few years, e-mail and the internet have revolutionised the way we communicate. From pensioners to pre-schoolers, people from all levels of society are familiar with e-mail and find it as comfortable as using the telephone.

The use of marine e-mail is also becoming extremely popular and has more or less replaced the use of telegrams and telex. However, the experience of using shoreside e-mail is quite unlike that of using most marine services, and this is because speeds are one or two orders of magnitude slower. There are exceptions, which we'll look at later in the chapter, but this effectively limits use to plain text documents only. Users sending messages to or from boats are strongly discouraged from using any procedure that unnecessarily increases the message size, including:

- Use of HTML, RTF or other document formats.
- Use of long signatures.
- Posting copies of the sender's original message along with the reply.
- Some systems are unable to handle file attachments but those that can suggest keeping them to a minimum and as small as possible.
- Signing up on mailing lists unless they are specifically designed for marine users.

Unfortunately, many people send e-mails with little idea of exactly what they are sending and are often unaware that they are using HTML or including heaps of hidden characters. Someone else set up their computer; they know only a limited range of commands and are afraid to change the program settings for fear they'll upset something and need to call a specialist to sort it out. If any of your correspondents fits this description, much frustration and heartache can be saved by making sure they are able to send plain text e-mails before your departure. Once the possibility of personal contact is lost, technical points are always so much more difficult to explain.

Most marine e-mail systems simply could not cope with the level of unsolicited 'junk' mailings that many shoreside users now accept as the norm. System operators may block messages that exceed a given size or, in some cases, only allow nominated addresses to forward mail to marine stations. To keep download times and service costs within reasonable limits, it's important to explain these limitations to your correspondents and ask them to consider holding back on any large postings until you can get to an internet café or other shoreside facility. A further point to bear in mind is that, unless your correspondence is encrypted, which is not permitted on amateur bands, it can easily be read by anyone listening in to the radio link.

Comparative speeds of marine and shoreside data services

Shoreside service	Typical speed (bps)	Mobile marine service	Typical speed (bps)
Dial up phone line	28,800	GTor	5 to 300
Broad band (Cable or ADSL)	840,000	Pactor 1	100 or 200
		Pactor 2	Up to 800
		Pactor 3	
		Cell Phone (GSM)	9,600
		Cell Phone (GPRS)	44,000
		Inmarsat Fleet F77	Up to 64,000

HF e-mail services

These offer the lowest cost and also the slowest services. Coverage is, in principle, worldwide but is always subject to the vagaries of HF propagation and relies on your provider having a station that you can contact. Some services sell or rent their own special modems but most can be accessed with one of the standard multipurpose data controllers described in the last chapter.

Similarly with software, some issue their own with custom facilities that exploit their own service but several make use of Airmail 2000, a program written by long-term cruiser and programmer Jim Corenman. Airmail 2000 is to marine e-mail what Microsoft's Outlook Express or Qualcomm's Eudora are to regular shoreside e-mail; it is the client side program in which you compose outgoing messages and store received mail. In addition to the usual e-mailer program features, eg in, out and

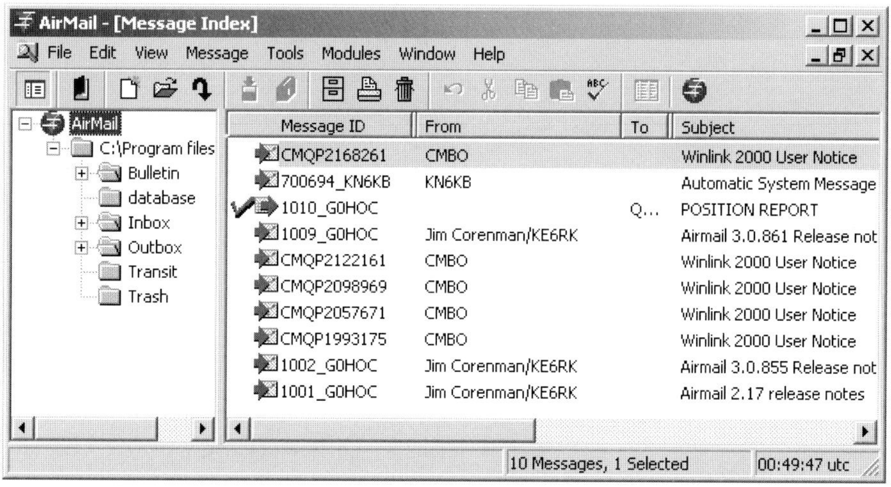

Fig 9.1 Airmail 2000 client side HF e-mail software main screen.

trash mailboxes and an address book, it includes several utilities:

- Telnet client – useful if you are in a marina with access to a regular phone line and need to clear your HF e-mails without actually using HF. The advantages are that it's faster and you don't cause interference to other boats close by.
- Can be used for conventional SMTP and POP3 e-mail services.
- HF propagation predictor.
- Maintains updated HF station frequency lists.
- Packet radio terminal program.

Airmail 2000 is free for amateur users and the latest updates can be downloaded from the Airmail 2000 web site (www.airmail2000.com). The site is well worth a visit for its sound advice for newcomers, in particular the 'Pactor Primer' page covering the fundamentals of using Pactor, installing a data controller and operational protocols.

In the remainder of this section, we will look a range of providers and the services they offer.

Sailmail (www.sailmail.com)

User hardware: Pactor data controller
User software: Airmail 2000
Data mode: Pactor 1 or 2
Coverage: Worldwide depending on contact with a participating radio station (see Fig 9.2).
Charges: Flat rate annual membership fee only.
Limitations: Open to vessels of less than 1600 gross registered tons. Ten minutes/day maximum connection time.

The Sailmail Association is a non-profit organisation established in 1997 by Stan Honey and aimed particularly at small craft. Members must be fully licensed to operate on HF marine bands and vessels must not be

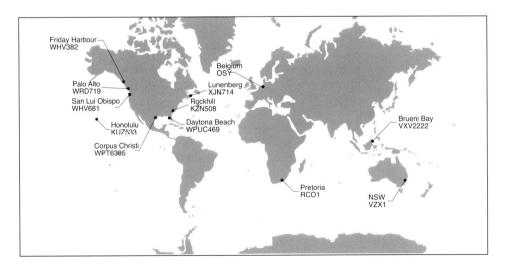

Fig 9.2 Sailmail stations around the world.

bigger than 1600 gross registered tons. Apart from a flat annual membership fee, there are no other fees to pay though daily connection times must not exceed ten minutes. At typical modem speeds this corresponds to between four and 50 typed A4 pages.

WinLink (www.winlink.org)

User hardware: Pactor data controller (excl. radio & computer)
User software: Airmail 2000
Data mode: Pactor 1 or 2
Coverage: Worldwide depending on contact with a participating radio station (see Fig 9.3).
Charges: Because this is an amateur service, there are no charges.
Limitations: Message content must comply with the conditions of the licence. This means that encryption is forbidden and in the US business correspondence is permitted only if neither party has a pecuniary interest. In most other countries all commercial traffic is forbidden.

The entire WinLink system, both hard and software, was developed, supported and maintained voluntarily by amateurs for use by other amateurs at no charge, and its success is a tribute to the teamwork of all involved. Around the world, a group of land based WinLink participating amateurs (PMBOs) have set up computer controlled radio stations with the sole purpose of processing e-mail traffic to and from users (see Fig 9.3). These fully automated stations routinely monitor set frequencies for incoming e-mail messages which, when received, are transferred to an internet mail server where they are then handled and delivered as a regular e-mail.

The PMBO is also in internet contact with the Winlink Central Mail Server (CMBO) in the US, which acts as a central clearing station for all e-mails addressed to amateur users. Each

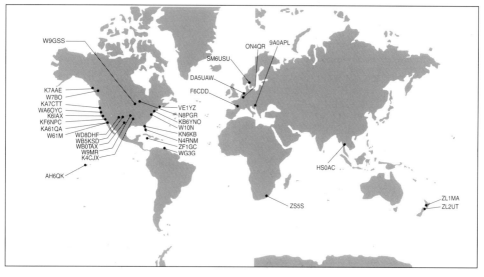

Fig 9.3 WinLink2000 PMBO HF stations around the world.

PMBO around the world holds a copy of every e-mail sent to a Winlink address and in this way the user is not committed to using a single PMBO, but can pick up mail from any that he/she is able to contact. Once downloaded the PMBO notifies the CMBO which, in turn, tells all other PMBOs that the particular message can be deleted.

MarineNet (www.MarineNet.net)

User hardware: (excl. radio & computer)	Pactor data controller upgraded with SCS Professional firmware.
User software:	Calypso e-mail client allowing use with SSB, satellite or wired connections with one e-mail program.
Data mode:	Pactor 2 & 3
Coverage:	Worldwide but depends on contact with a participating radio station in the network. At present there are two stations; one in the US, in Florida, and one in Kiel, Germany, with several more to come online in mid 2002 in New Zealand, Seattle WA. and Texas.
Charges:	A flat fee for flexible access period. There are no charges for traffic. Service can be suspended while off the vessel.
Limitations:	The connection time allowance is ten hours per month, however additional monthly time may be purchased. Outside of this there are no daily limits.

MarineNet operate their own web/mail servers and provide users with their own POP mailbox and marine SMTP services. Both server and client side software have been written with marine users in mind and special attention paid to reducing download times. These benefits also extend to users of their integrated satellite service.

The company also offer a range of hardware packages which should greatly relieve the incompatibility and set-up difficulties that can frequently occur when you bring together parts from different suppliers.

Globe Wireless (www.globewireless.com)

User hardware: (computer)	Custom built Globe Wireless modem. Most modern marine radios are suitable but must have a software control interface.
User software:	Provided by Globe Wireless.
Data mode:	Globe Wireless proprietary standard capable of speeds comparable with current generation satellite systems.
Coverage:	Worldwide. There are 25 Globe Wireless HF stations throughout the world. The network is closely integrated with satellite systems that can be used if HF conditions are unworkable.
Charges:	A wide selection of billing schemes can be arranged to suit individual needs. Costs are reduced for bulk users but deals include a flat installation fee plus service

or yearly service contract with single billing.

Limitations: It may be difficult to use the equipment to access services that are not provided by Globe Wireless.

Globe Wireless is the largest provider of marine HF data services, and serves the needs of high volume commercial users. Their design philosophy is to build hard- and software that is as simple to operate as possible. With the emphasis on total software control that handles all transmit/receive switching and frequency changing, there is little need for users to be involved with radio operations. When HF conditions are poor, communications can be switched though satellite systems which are a closely integrated part of the Globe Wireless network.

Installation can be carried out either by the company's world mobile team of installers, or can sometimes be carried out by an approved local marine electronics engineer.

Beyond supplying the communications hard and software, the Globe Wireless aim is to provide a one-stop shop for all marine information needs; from weather and navigational data to ship and cargo tracking.

FTPMail-web access by e-mail

HF services are generally far too slow for web browsing so are usually limited to e-mail only though that is not quite the end of the story. Some major web servers provide a service known as FTPmail. This is a tool that allows plain text web pages to be captured as e-mail texts and is perfect for low bandwidth connections.

The US National Weather Service (NWS) site has FTPMail and is well documented and a good example of its use. To use it, you send a subjectless text e-mail to ftpmail@weather. noaa. gov and in the body of the message you enter a list of commands. There are a couple of examples on the following page:

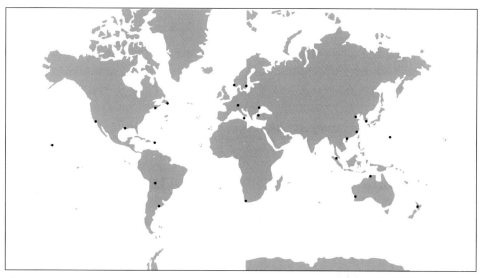

Fig 9.4 Globe Wireless marine network stations.

To:	ftpmail@weather.noaa.gov
Subject:	
Body:	Help

The message above retrieves the FTPMail help file containing detailed information on use of the system and command syntax. Now let's try something a little more rewarding:

For current lists of other servers with FTPMail facilities, enter FTPMail in your favourite search engine and you should find links to a couple of dozen or more.

To:	ftpmail@weather.noaa.gov
Subject:	
Body:	open iwin.nws.noaa.gov
	cd data
	cd text
	cd FZNT01
	get KWBC.TXT
	quit

The first line of this script opens the NWS default site, the next three lines step down through the date, text and FZNT01 subdirectories. Line five retrieves the KWBC.TXT file and line six closes the connection. In this case, in a few minutes you are e-mailed back with a copy of the current North Atlantic High Seas forecast. See the help file for details of other weather files available from this server.

UU encoding

FTPMail can be used to download files other than plain text; in fact any kind of binary file including spreadsheets and pictures can be accessed. The process used is called UU Encoding and converts each binary character into a series of printable characters that can be sent as a regular text e-mail. There is a short sample below:

```
begin 666 flatpan.zip
M4$L$#!!!0``````(````(`,``````@M@``M(`.,M`````+8`````````````
M4$L#!!!0`````@M@``M(`S.,Z`````@M`M`M`M`M`````````````
M4$L#BBbegin 666 flatpan.zip
M4$L#.....
&;PH`````
```

```
begin 666 flatpan.zip
M4$L#!!!0``````(````(`,```````@M
M5%/7%L://%%`48$OD$$$O)(2$(#-#@@@@MMMMM:$v9`$v$@vmmmm:"5("i8<*c:pvo8
Mjxg,H-Y`$*'5AyOhxe,O"(4xu1%9:-4@^m1g+5+?:k6uy]v[wogsw+/w_k[?
M``````````(`"v@0````!F;&%t7w!a;byg:6902p4&`````$``0`z````
&;ph`````
```

```
&;PH`````
```

```
end
```

To:	ftpmail@weather.noaa.gov
Subject:	
Body:	open
	cd fax
	get PWAE98.TIF
	quit

Many e-mail client programs (eg Eudora) handle UU encoding without the user even knowing it's happening but if yours does not, you'll need to decode it as a separate operation. WinZip (available from www.winzip.com) has the ability to unscramble UU encoded files and is a useful utility to have aboard even if you don't use it for this purpose.

The above example shows the syntax for downloading PWAE98.TIF, which is a North Atlantic wind/wave chart. Once decoded, you'll need a TIF file viewer to see the chart.

Finally, an important point to remember about UU encoding is that it makes files bigger so they take longer to send than their byte count would indicate. It would not be suitable for sending large bitmap pictures of the family. However, for smaller files, in a compact graphics format (eg GIF or JPG) or if compressed with WinZip, it is ideal.

YOTREPS passage reports

YOTREPS is a voluntary reporting scheme that uses e-mail to forward daily positions and weather observations from boats on passage. Reports are forwarded to weather forecasters, who use them as a check on atmospheric modelling and thus help to improve the accuracy of future forecasts. They're also forwarded to search and rescue co-ordinators, where they contribute to a plot of all known vessels in their coverage area. In an emergency, this enables them to track not only a particular boat in difficulties but also others in the area that may be able to assist. Further benefits to participants include:

• A personalised web page showing a plot of your last 30 reports within the last year. See Fig 9.5 for an example.
• Reports contribute to a database of passage weather observations for analysis of trends in ocean cruising weather conditions. Where there is sufficient data, the YOTREPS web site includes a page providing a historical review of conditions experienced on popular cruising routes during specified months.
• In some areas, forecasters feed back long term weather prognoses for boats transiting their area.
• Boats can obtain e-mailed report summaries from other boats in their area that can be plotted to show their position, course and wind vectors.
• The service is available to amateurs and non-amateurs alike (www.pangolin.co.nz).

Submitting YOTREPS reports

YOTREPS reports are sent as plain text e-mails but for boats that do not have e-mail capabilities all is not lost. Some radio nets (eg Pacific Seafarer's net page 161) routinely forward

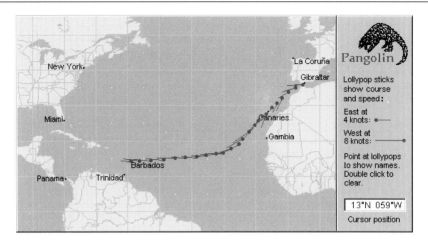

Fig 9.5 YOTREPS web site plot of the vessel *Gambor* on passage between Gibraltar and Martinique via Gran Canaria. (See more plots on www.pangolin.co.nz/yotreps/reporter_list.asp)

reports on behalf of the boats checking in. Also, if you are sailing as part of a group, it may be possible to pass report details by radio to another member of the group for forwarding.

Because they are machine read, adherence to a standard format is essential. They are prepared as plain text e-mails as in the following example:

The YOTREPS Reporter

Another technique for formatting reports is to use the Reporter program that's available as a free download from the YOTREPS web site. As with Airmail 2000, it includes a form for entering position and weather observations and then the details are assembled into a correctly formatted text e-mail, ready for

```
YOTREPS
13/03/2002

                                | BOAT  |  WIND  |  SWELL |     |     |      |
   No | CALL   |TIME  |  POSITION     |Cse|Spd|       |       |Cld |Bar  |tend |
      |        | UTC  | Lat.    Lng   |d T|Kts|Dir|Kts|Dir| Ht| %  | hPa|      |
   ---|--------|----- |---------------|---|---|---|---|---|---|----|-----|----- |
    1 |Gambor  |1717  |15 56 N 083 44 W|284|6.0|E  |010| NE|0.6|20  |1016|  +2 |
```

Lines 3, 4, 5 & 6 are optional but the formatting and content of the other three are critical. In principle, reports could be compiled and sent by typing the above into a simple e-mail text editor, but if you're using Airmail 2000 an easier way is to use the included YOTREPS report form. The job is then reduced to simply filling in the boxes.

dispatch. It also has the ability to produce block reports from a number of boats and has a world coastal outline chart screen on which positions are plotted, along with course and speed and wind vectors (see Fig 9.6).

The chart is backed by a database of 4500 marked ports and anchorages with names that can be displayed at will; a plotting tool

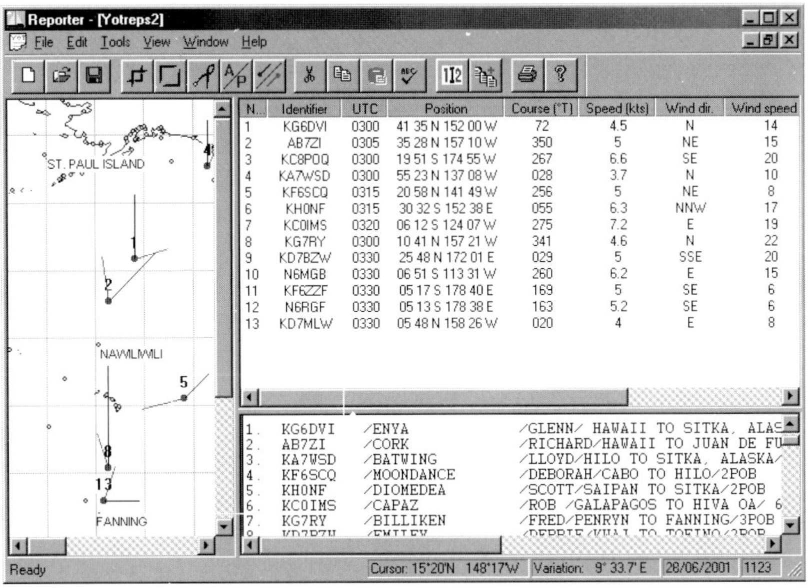

Fig 9.6 The YOTREPS Reporter showing a block report from the Pacific Seafarer's net. The 13 boats listed have sent their reports by SSB phone and the net has forwarded them as an e-mail. The plot shows a small group en route between Hawaii and Alaska.

for measuring and drawing Great Circle courses and distances; and a magnetic variation calculator that shows current values for anywhere in the world.

Plotting reports from other boats in your area

YOTREPS reporting is a two way process and by completing a web site form you can arrange to be e-mailed daily report summaries from other boats. These arrive in the regular YOTREPS report format and the file can be loaded back into the Reporter to display a plot of other boats in your area along with their speed and wind vectors. For boats on passage, this is useful strategic information giving advanced warning of other boats you may come close to, perhaps at

night, and of weather conditions experienced by those around you.

YOTREPS weathergrams

Cruising boats frequently visit parts of the world that are not on regular shipping routes and where there are few weather reporting stations. Reliable reports of actual weather conditions are of special interest to forecasters as they help confirm or deny the accuracy of theoretical predictions. Some forecast agencies, notably New Zealand Metservice and MCS Marine in the UK, provide long term weather prospects for vessels in their coverage area, in plain text format. As with the boat report summaries, boats on passage can choose to receive these by e-mail as and when they are issued.

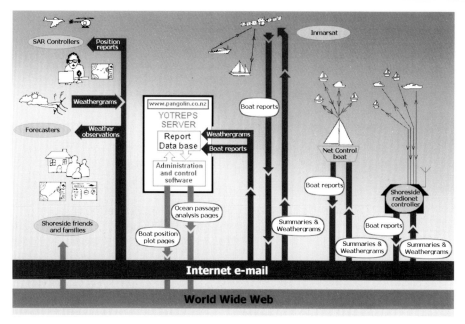

Fig 9.7 YOTREPS reports are shared between boats, shoreside forecasters, SAR co-ordinators and shoreside friends and family.

Full internet access

Internet access for web browsing, viewing pictures or charts, or downloading software still remains an elusive goal for most marine users. Of the systems available that can provide it, all have serious drawbacks; GPRS cell phones give only local coverage and although Inmarsat-B, F77 or F55 have the technical capabilities, only a few are able to afford them. At some stage these barriers are sure to be broken and, rather in the way that the internet has permanently changed so many aspects of life and work ashore, seafarers can expect similar fundamental changes to the daily routine.

So, for the foreseeable future, or until the emergence of effective competition, a strong need for many old services will remain. Slow data connections, fine for basic text e-mail, could take an hour to download the graphics file equivalent of a Weatherfax page and even longer for satellite images. There still seems to be a reasonable future for Weatherfax and satellite reception gear and although weather information is of vital importance to seafarers, its provision by these means is not covered by the GMDSS. Without this incentive to continue, and given a policy of 'user pays', it is unclear how much longer many of the agencies that currently provide fax and satellite images will be able to continue.

PART TWO

1 • Procedures, protocols and codes

Non-GMDSS Distress, Urgency and Safety signals

Distress (MAYDAY)

The international radiotelephone frequencies for distress calls are: 2182, 4125, 6215, 8291, 12 290, 16 420kHz in the MF/HF marine bands; Channel 16 156.800MHz in the VHF marine band. **Speak slowly and distinctly.**

the call, you must do so. Then call a Coastguard station or a coastal station with the details.

The word MAYDAY should only be spoken over the radio as part of a distress call.

Urgency (PAN PAN)

Use any of the international radiotelephone distress frequencies.

MAYDAY MAYDAY MAYDAY	Pronounced as in the French word *m'aider*.
THIS IS	Name of vessel and call sign three times.
THIS IS	
THIS IS	
MAYDAY	Name of vessel and call sign once.
MY POSITION IS	Latitude/longitude position or the true bearing and distance from a known position.

The Distress signal is used to indicate:

'Grave and imminent danger to a ship, aircraft, vehicle or person, requiring immediate assistance.'

Use of this signal imposes general radio silence, which is maintained until the emergency is over. If you hear a Distress call, write down the details. If no one else answers

The Urgency signal indicates a **very urgent** message concerning the safety of a ship, aircraft or other vehicle, or the safety of a person as in the case of serious injury or loss overboard. You would normally expect an immediate response. The message is in a similar format to a Distress call. If you hear an Urgency call you should respond in the same way as for a Distress call (see panel overleaf).

PAN PAN PAN PAN PAN PAN	Pronounced as in the French word *panne*.
HELLO ALL STATIONS HELLO ALL STATIONS HELLO ALL STATIONS	Or name of a specific station.
THIS IS .... THIS IS .... THIS IS	Name of vessel and call sign three times.
MY POSITION IS	As for MAYDAY.
....	Nature of the emergency and assistance required.

Safety

The radiotelephone Safety signal consists of the French word *sécurité*, pronounced Say-cur-e-tay, said three times. It indicates a message about the safety of navigation generally, such as a drifting light buoy, a wreck, a failed light or gale warnings. Such messages usually originate ashore, but they should be used by ships at sea to report a navigational hazard.

Safety messages are normally transmitted on working channels after an initial announcement on the calling channel.

Requesting assistance

Calling for assistance is never a step that should be taken without consideration for the possible consequences. For example, a simple request for a tow into harbour from a passing vessel could be viewed quite differently after the event by those rendering the service. What, at the time, seemed an amicable arrangement, could later be presented as plucking you from impending disaster, or from certain destruction on nearby rocks in mounting sea conditions. The assisting crew's objective might be to substantiate a large claim for salvage, which in some parts of the world is a common occurrence. It is an art that some are well versed in and they are ready to exploit any language difficulties or evidence of incompetence. To reduce your exposure to these risks:

- Never request assistance unless it is absolutely necessary.
- Always agree on a price for the job in advance, preferably in writing.
- Log all operational events, details and agreements and have the log signed by witnesses as to its veracity.
- Always maintain command and control of the whole operation.
- For tows, use your own tow rope whenever possible.
- Try to maintain radio contact with others that are following the situation.

If the assistance is offered for salvage only, be sure that the services are under the terms of the normal Lloyd's open 'Standard Form' with the principle of 'No Cure – No Pay'. A simplified version of the form is presented here on a page that can be torn out for rapid use.

Full copies of the Lloyd's Open Form Salvage Agreement can be obtained from the Salvage Arbitration Branch, Lloyd's of London, www.lloyds.com lloyds-salvage@lloyds.com.

A Simple Form of Salvage Agreement

'NO CURE – NO PAY'

(From the *The Yachtsman's Lawyer* (RYA) Edmund Whelan incorporating Lloyd's Open Form)

On board the Yacht: .... Date: ....

IT IS HEREBY AGREED BETWEEN: ....

for and on behalf of the owners of the ....
(Hereinafter called 'the Owners')

AND for and on behalf of: ....
(Hereinafter called 'the Contractor')

1 That the Contractor will use his best endeavours to salve the ... .
and take her into .... or such other place as may hereinafter be agreed or if no place is named or agreed to a place of safety.
2 That the services shall be rendered by the Contractor and accepted by the owner as salvage services upon the principle of 'No Cure – No Pay' subject to the terms conditions and provisions (including those relating to Arbitration and providing of security) of the current Standard Form of Salvage Agreement approved and published by the Council of Lloyd's of London and known as Lloyd's Open Form.
3 In the event of success the Contractor's remuneration shall be .... or if no sum be mutually agreed between the parties or entered herein the same shall be fixed by arbitration in London in the manner prescribed in Lloyd's Open Form.
4 The Owners their servants and agents shall cooperate fully with the contractor in and about the salvage including obtaining entry to the place named in Clause 1 hereof or the place of safety. The Contractor may make reasonable use of the vessel's machinery gear equipment anchors chains stores and other appurtenances during and for the purpose of the services free of expense but shall not unnecessarily damage abandon or sacrifice the same or any property the subject of this Agreement.

For and on behalf of the Owners of property to be salved:

....

For and on behalf of the Contractor:

....

Reporting marine weather

It's surprising how a report of even the simplest observations can be open to a variety of interpretations. When talking about the date and time, for example, do we mean the local time with any adjustment for daylight saving, or perhaps Zone, or Universal time? If we specify a compass course, do we give what the compass actually reads or is it corrected for the local magnetic variation? When reporting boat speed, would that be our speed through the water or the speed over the sea bed? When exchanging information between people from different backgrounds, cultures and experience, it is absolutely essential to be sure that we are speaking the same language. Fortunately, with marine weather reporting, there is already a widely used, internationally agreed standard that has been in regular use for many decades.

The World Meteorological Organization (WMO) Voluntary Observing Ship scheme (VOS) uses a system of encoding (BBXX) that firmly defines the parameters to be given in weather reports. It is these, with some small noted differences, that are used in YOTREPS reports and are as follows:

Parameter	Units	Explanation	Note
Date and Time	UTC	UTC (Co-ordinated Universal Time) which for this purpose is synonymous with GMT (Greenwich Mean Time)	
Position	Degrees and minutes	Report positions using separate single digits only. Give the latitude as two digits of degrees followed by two digits of minutes followed by the name (ie north or south). Give longitude as three digits of degrees followed by two digits of minutes followed by the name (ie east or west). For example, a position of 28 degrees 5 minutes north; 45 degrees 17 minutes east would be read out as: *'Two eight degrees, zero five minutes north, zero four five degrees, one seven minutes east'.*	1
Boat course	Degrees true	Boat's course through the water (not necessarily the same as the boat's heading).	2
Boat speed	Knots	Average speed over the last three hours to the nearest whole number. Speed reported should be the speed over the ground.	3
Wind direction	Compass points or degrees true	Direction of the true wind. To obtain this use either the Beaufort scale or correct the masthead wind indicator reading for the boat's speed and course.	

Parameter	Units	Explanation	Note
Wind speed	Knots	Average speed of the true wind. To obtain this use either the Beaufort scale or correct the masthead wind indicator reading for the boat's speed and course.	
Swell direction	Compass points or degrees true	Direction of the main ocean swell.	
Swell height	Metres	Vertical distance from trough to crest and the average of the larger well formed swells.	
Cloud cover	%	Proportion of the sky covered by cloud.	4
Pressure	Hpa	Barometric pressure.	
Pressure tendency	+ or − hPa	Pressure change over the past three hours. Prefix with a plus or minus sign to indicate rising or falling. Report 0 if steady.	

Notes

1 The style *twenty-eight* degrees *five* minutes *north*, *forty-five* degrees *seventeen* minutes *east* is a little shorter but is more difficult to understand over a poor radio link and should not be used. Never use the word 'decimal' or 'point' to separate the degrees from the minutes field. This implies that the position is given in degrees and decimal degrees; an alternative format widely used in marine forecasts.

2 The course reported should be obtained by correcting the compass heading for deviation, magnetic variation and leeway and drift.

3 Except when in a strong current, which is unusual on an ocean passage, speed over the ground will be very similar to speed through the water and could be measured by electric or mechanical log, GPS set or visual estimate. Remember to report the average and not peaks that might occur when surfing down wave fronts.

4 To estimate cloud cover, imagine the sky divided into quarters like a cake. Imagine each quarter further divided into two parts; each segment forming one eighth of the total sky. These are known as *oktas* and are the unit of cloud cover used by professional observers. Perhaps because the okta is not widely familiar, cloud cover is often reported as a percentage. Multiply the number of oktas by 12.5 to convert to a percentage.

The standard phonetic alphabet and numerals

Letter	Pronunciation	Letter	Pronunciation
A alfa	Alfah	N november	noVEMber
B bravo	BRAHvoh	O oscar	OSScar
C charlie	CHARlee	P papa	pahPAH
D delta	DELLtah	Q quebec	kehBECK
E echo	ECKoh	R romeo	ROWmeoh
F foxtrot	FOKStrot	S sierra	seeAIRrah
G golf	Golf	T tango	TANGgo
H hotel	hohTELL	U uniform	YOUneeform
I india	INdeeah	V victor	VIKtah
J juliet	JEWleeEtt	W whiskey	WISSkey
K kilo	KEYloh	X x-ray	ECKSray
L lima	LEEmah	Y yankee	YANGkey
M mike	Mike	Z zulu	ZOOloo

Figure	Pronunciation	Figure	Pronunciation
1	Wun	6	Six
2	Too	7	SEV-en
3	Tree	8	Ait
4	FOW-er	9	NIN-er
5	Fife	0	Zero

Morse code

Morse has been abandoned as an official method for communicating at sea although it is still in use by radio amateurs and is likely to remain in use long after it has been dropped as a licence requirement.

Readability depends upon good timing and although it may be sent at various speeds, it is important that the correct time relationships are maintained. The duration of the dash, and the intervals between characters and between words should be related to the duration of the dot as follows:

Dash period:	3 x dot period
Space between characters: (within a single letter or number):	1 dot period
Space between letters or numbers:	3 x dot period
Space between words:	greater than 5 x dot period

Letter	Code	Letter	Code
A	• —	S	• • •
B	— • • •	T	—
C	— • — •	U	• • —
D	— • •	V	• • • —
E	•	W	• —
F	• • — •	X	— • • —
G	— — •	Y	— • — —
H	• • • •	Z	— — • •
I	• •	1	• — — — —
J	• — — —	2	• • — — —
K	— • —	3	• • • — —
L	• — • •	4	• • • • —
M	— —	5	• • • • •
N	— •	6	— • • • •
O	— — —	7	— — • • •
P	• — — •	8	— — — • •
Q	— — • —	9	— — — — •
R	• — •	0	— — — — —

Letter	Code	Accented letter	Code
Full stop(.)	• — • — • —	À, á, â	• — — • —
Comma (,)	— — • • — —	Ä	• — • —
Colon(:)	— — — • •	ç	— • — • •
Question mark (?)	• • — — • •	È, é	• • — • •
Apostrophe (')	• — — — — •	ê	— • • — •
Hyphen(-)	— • • • • —	ñ	— — • — —
Fraction bar (/)	— • • — •	ö	— — — •
Brackets – open (()	— • — — •	ü	• • — —
Brackets – close ())	— • — — • —		
Double hyphen (=)	— • • • —		
Quotation marks (")	• — • • — •		
Error	• • • • • •		

On the island of La Gomera in the Canaries, local people amaze visitors with their ancient traditional skill for whistling messages across deep valleys. Even quite complex messages can be passed over distances far too great for shouting. Now with Morse code you can do the same. Use it with a conch shell to signal to your crew on the beach to bring more beer.

Extracts from the international Q code

The value of these codes is that they are widely understood across language barriers. They can be used as both statements or as questions by adding a question mark and can be spelt out phonetically or sent in Morse. Some have even been incorporated as procedure codes in automatic telex machines.

Code	Meaning
QRA	What is the name of your vessel (or station)?
	The name of my vessel (or station) is ...
QRB	How far approximately are you from my station?
	The approximate distance between our stations is ... nautical miles (or kilometres).
QRG	Will you tell me my exact frequency (or that of ...)
	Your exact frequency (or that of ...) is ... MHz (or kHz).
QRH	Does my frequency vary?
	Your frequency varies.
QRL	Are you busy?
	I am busy (or I am busy with ...(name/callsign)). Please do not interfere.

Code	Meaning
QRM	Are you being interfered with?
	I am being interfered with.
QRN	Are you troubled by static?
	I am troubled by static.
QRO	Shall I increase transmitter power?
	Increase transmitter power.
QRP	Shall I decrease transmitter power?
	Decrease transmitter power.
QRQ	Shall I send faster?
	Send faster (... words per minute).
QRS	Shall I send more slowly?
	Send more slowly (... words per minute).
QRT	Shall I stop sending?
	Stop sending.
QRW	Shall I inform ... that you will call him on ... MHz (or kHz)?
	Please inform ... that I am calling him/her on ... MHz (or kHz).
QRX	When will you call me again?
	I will call you again at ... hours on ... MHz (or kHz).
QRZ	Who is calling me?
	Your are being called by ... on ... MHz (or kHz).
QSA	What is the strength of my signals (or those of ... (name/callsign))?
	The strength of your signals (or those of ...) is ... (see page 138).
QSB	Are my signals fading?
	Your signals are fading.
QSK	Can you hear me between your signals and if so can I break in on your transmission?
	I can hear you between my signals; break in on my transmission.
QSL	Can you acknowledge receipt?
	I acknowledge receipt.
QSP	Will you relay to ... (name/callsign) free of charge?
	I will relay to ... (name/callsign) free of charge.
QSQ	Have you a doctor on board (or is ... (name of person) on board)?
	I have a doctor on board (or ... (name of person) is on board).
QSO	Can you communicate with ... (name/callsign) direct (or by relay)?
	I can communicate with ... (name/callsign) direct (or by relay through ...).
QST	Is there a message for all stations?
	Here follows a message for all stations ...

Code	Meaning
QSY	Shall I change to transmission on another frequency?
	Change to transmission on another frequency (or on ... MHz (or kHz)).
QTE	What is my true bearing from you? OR What is my true bearing from ... (name/callsign) OR What is the true bearing of (name/callsign) from ... (name/callsign).
	Your true bearing from me is ... degrees at ... hours. OR Your true bearing from (name/callsign) was ... degrees at ... hours. OR The true bearing of ... (name/callsign) from ... (name/callsign) was ... degrees at ... hours.
QTH	What is your position in latitude/longitude (or according to any other indication?
	My position is ... latitude ... longitude (or according to any other indication).
QTI	What is your true course?
	My true course is ... degrees.
QTJ	What is your speed? (ie speed of a ship or aircraft through the water or air respectively)
	My speed is ... knots (OR kilometres per hour OR statute miles per hour).
QTL	What is your true heading?
	My true heading is ... degrees.
QTM	What is your magnetic heading?
	My magnetic heading is ... degrees.
QTR	What is the correct time?
	The correct time is ... hours.

Telex codes and abbreviations

Service codes	
BRK+	Break, ie breaks the connection with the remote station
DIRTLX...+	Direct telex
FAX+	Store and forward facsimile
GA+	Go ahead, ie go ahead and transmit
HELP+	Request a list of services and codes
KKKK	Breaks the connection (sent by the remote station)
NNNN	End of message
MED+	Request for medical advice or assistance
MSG+	Please send any traffic that you have on hand for me
OBS+	Weather observation message
OPR+	Request for operator assistance
RTL+	Radio telex
TLX ...+	Store and forward telex

Abbreviations	
BK	Break
CFM	Confirm
COL	Collate
DER	Out of order
EEE	Error
INF	Contact information
MIN	Minutes
MOM	Please wait
MSG	Message
NC	No line available
OCC	Occupied – terminal busy
OK	Agreed
PLS	Please
PPR	Paper
QSL	Receipt acknowledged
R	Received
RAP	I will call again
RPT	Please repeat
TAX	What is the charge?
THRU	You are connected – please go ahead
WRU	Who are you?

The RST code

This code is used for reporting the quality of signals in terms of their readability (R), and strength (S). (The 'T' refers to the tone of Morse signals on a scale of 1 to 9.) As an example, a perfectly readable, exceptionally strong signal would be reported as 'five and nine'.

Readability

Code	Description
R1	Unreadable
R2	Barely readable, occasional words distinguishable
R3	Readable with considerable difficulty
R4	Readable with practically no difficulty
R5	Perfectly readable

Signal Strength

Code	Description
S1	Faint signals, barely perceptible
S2	Very weak signals
S3	Weak signals
S4	Fair signals
S5	Fairly good signals
S6	Good signals
S7	Moderately strong signals
S8	Strong signals
S9	Exceptionally strong signals

Transmitter power is not everything

Most communications receivers have a meter that measures the strength of incoming signals. It is usually calibrated in 'S' points; 1 S point being approximately 3dB (see page 166) and corresponding to a transmitted power reduction of 50 per cent. From the above table it can be seen that this large drop in power corresponds to a relatively small drop in perceived signal strength, the difference between an 'exceptionally strong' and 'strong' signal.

Maritime Mobile Service Identifiers (MMSI)

These are included within the 9 digit MMSI and indicate the issuing authority (see page 25 for make-up of the MMSI).

MID	Name
501	Adelie Land
401	Afghanistan
303	Alaska
201	Albania
605	Algeria
559	American Samoa
202	Andorra
603	Angola
301	Anguilla
304	Antigua and Barbuda
701	Argentine Republic
307	Aruba
608	Ascension Island
503	Australia
203	Austria
423	Azerbaijani Republic
204	Azores
308–309, 311	Bahamas
408	Bahrain
405	Bangladesh
314	Barbados
206	Belarus

MID	Name
205	Belgium
312	Belize
610	Benin
310	Bermuda
410	Bhutan
720	Bolivia
611	Botswana
710	Brazil
378	British Virgin Islands
508	Brunei Darussalam
207	Bulgaria
633	Burkina Faso
609	Burundi
514	Cambodia
613	Cameroon
316	Canada
617	Cape Verde
319	Cayman Islands
612	Central African Republic
670	Chad
725	Chile
412, 413	China
516	Christmas Island (Indian Ocean)
523	Cocos (Keeling) Islands
730	Colombia
616	Comoros
615	Congo
518	Cook Islands
321	Costa Rica
619	Côte d'Ivoire
238	Croatia
618	Crozet Archipelago
323	Cuba
209, 210, 212	Cyprus
270	Czech Republic
445	Democratic People's Republic of Korea

MID	Name
676	Democratic Republic of the Congo
219, 220	Denmark
621	Djibouti
325	Dominica
327	Dominican Republic
735	Ecuador
622	Egypt
359	El Salvador
631	Equatorial Guinea
625	Eritrea
276	Estonia
624	Ethiopia
740	Falkland Islands (Malvinas)
231	Faroe Islands
520	Fiji
230	Finland
226, 227, 228	France
546	French Polynesia
626	Gabonese Republic
629	Gambia
213	Georgia
211, 218	Germany
627	Ghana
236	Gibraltar
237, 239	Greece
331	Greenland
330	Grenada
329	Guadeloupe
332	Guatemala
745	Guiana
632	Guinea
630	Guinea-Bissau
750	Guyana
336	Haiti
334	Honduras
477	Hong Kong
243	Hungary

MID	Name
251	Iceland
419	India
525	Indonesia
422	Iran
425	Iraq
250	Ireland
428	Israel
247	Italy
339	Jamaica
431, 432	Japan
438	Jordan
436	Kazakstan
634	Kenya
635	Kerguelen Islands
529	Kiribati
440, 441	Korea
447	Kuwait
531	Lao People's Democratic Republic
275	Latvia
450	Lebanon
644	Lesotho
636	Liberia
642	Libya
252	Liechtenstein
277	Lithuania
253	Luxembourg
453	Macao
647	Madagascar
255	Madeira
655	Malawi
533	Malaysia
455	Maldives
649	Mali
215, 256, 248-249	Malta
538	Marshall Islands
347	Martinique

MID	Name
654	Mauritania
645	Mauritius
345	Mexico
510	Micronesia
214	Moldova
254	Monaco
457	Mongolia
348	Montserrat
242	Morocco
650	Mozambique
506	Myanmar
659	Namibia
544	Nauru
459	Nepal
244, 245, 246	Netherlands
306	Netherlands Antilles
540	New Caledonia
512	New Zealand
350	Nicaragua
656	Niger
657	Nigeria
542	Niue
536	Northern Mariana Islands
257, 258, 259	Norway
461	Oman
463	Pakistan
511	Palau
351–357	Panama
553	Papua New Guinea
755	Paraguay
760	Peru
548	Philippines
555	Pitcairn Island
261	Poland
263	Portugal
358	Puerto Rico
466	Qatar
660	Reunion

MID	Name
264	Romania
273	Russian Federation
661	Rwandese Republic
665	Saint Helena
341	Saint Kitts and Nevis
343	Saint Lucia
607	Saint Paul and Amsterdam Islands
361	Saint Pierre and Miquelon
375–376	Saint Vincent and the Grenadines
561	Samoa
268	San Marino
668	Sao Tome and Principe
403	Saudi Arabia
663	Senegal
664	Seychelles
667	Sierra Leone
563–564	Singapore
267	Slovak Republic
278	Slovenia
557	Solomon Islands
666	Somali Democratic Republic
601	South Africa
224	Spain
417	Sri Lanka
662	Sudan
765	Suriname
669	Swaziland
265	Sweden
269	Switzerland
468	Syrian Arab Republic

MID	Name
416	Taiwan
674	Tanzania
677	Tanzania
567	Thailand
274	The Former Yugoslav Republic of Macedonia
671	Togolese Republic
570	Tonga
362	Trinidad and Tobago
672	Tunisia
271	Turkey
434	Turkmenistan
364	Turks and Caicos Islands
572	Tuvalu
675	Uganda
272	Ukraine
470	United Arab Emirates
232–235	United Kingdom of Great Britain and Northern Ireland
338, 366–369	United States of America
379	United States Virgin Islands
770	Uruguay
576	Vanuatu
208	Vatican City State
775	Venezuela
574	Vietnam
578	Wallis and Futuna Islands
473, 475	Yemen
279	Yugoslavia
678	Zambia
679	Zimbabwe

2 • Frequency allocations

Marine MF/HF – SSB channels and frequencies

All transmissions are upper side band.

Channel no	Ship transmit	Ship receive
201	2430	2572
209	2031.5	2490
221	2118	2514
228	2155.5	1620.5
232	2166	2558
242	2003	2450
242	2366	2450
245	2390	2566
247	2406	2442
248	2406	2506
401	4065	4357
402	4068	4360
403	4071	4363
404	4074	4366
405	4077	4369
406	4080	4372
407	4083	4375
408	4086	4378
409	4089	4381
410	4092	4384
411	4095	4387
412	4098	4390
413	4101	4393
414	4104	4396
414	4179	4216.5

Channel no	Ship transmit	Ship receive
414	4166.5	4259
414	4154.5	4300.4
414	4157.5	4347
415	4107	4399
416	4110	4402
417	4113	4405
418	4116	4408
419	4119	4411
420	4122	4414
421	4125	4417
422	4128	4420
423	4131	4423
424	4134	4426
425	4137	4429
426	4140	4432
427	4143	4435
428	4060	4351
450	4215	*Distress*
451	4146	Simplex
452	4149	Simplex
453	4417	Simplex
650	6215	*Distress*
651	6224	Simplex
652	6227	Simplex
653	6230	Simplex

Channel no	Ship transmit	Ship receive
654	6516	Simplex
801	8195	8719
802	8198	8722
803	8201	8725
804	8204	8728
805	8207	8731
805	8379	8419
806	8210	8734
807	8213	8737
808	8216	8740
809	8219	8743
810	8222	8746
811	8225	8749
812	8228	8752
813	8231	8755
813	8382.5	8422.5
814	8234	8758
815	8237	8761
816	8240	8764
816	8384	8424
817	8243	8767
818	8246	8770
819	8249	8773
819	8385.5	8425.5
820	8252	8776
821	8255	8779
821	8386.5	8426.5
822	8258	8782
822	8387	8427
823	8261	8785
824	8264	8788
825	8267	8791
826	8270	8794
827	8273	8797
828	8276	8800
829	8279	8803

Channel no	Ship transmit	Ship receive
830	8282	8806
831	8285	8809
832	8288	8812
836	8113	8713
836	8394	8434
850	8291	*Distress*
851	8294	Simplex
852	8297	Simplex
1201	12230	13077
1202	12233	13080
1203	12236	13083
1204	12239	13086
1205	12242	13089
1206	12245	13092
1206	12479.5	12582
1207	12248	13095
1208	12251	13098
1209	12254	13101
1210	12257	13104
1210	12481.5	12584
1211	12260	13107
1212	12263	13110
1213	12266	13113
1213	12483	12585.5
1214	12269	13116
1215	12272	13119
1216	12275	13122
1217	12278	13125
1218	12281	13128
1219	12284	13131
1219	12486	12588.5
1220	12287	13134
1221	12290	13137
1221	12487	12589.5
1222	12293	13140
1223	12296	13143

Channel no	Ship transmit	Ship receive
1224	12299	13146
1225	12302	13149
1226	12305	13152
1227	12308	13155
1228	12311	13158
1229	12314	13161
1229	12491	12593.5
1230	12317	13164
1231	12320	13167
1232	12323	13170
1233	12326	13173
1235	12332	13179
1242	12497.5	12600
1244	12498.5	12601
1247	12500	12602.5
1250	12290	*Distress*
1251	12353	Simplex
1252	12356	Simplex
1253	12359	Simplex
1257	12505	12607.5
1263	12508	12610.5
1265	12509	12611.5
1291	12522	12624
1301	12527	12629
1301	12373.5	12668
1601	16360	17242
1602	16363	17245
1603	16366	17248
1604	16369	17251
1605	16372	17254
1606	16375	17257
1606	16686	16809.5
1607	16378	17260
1608	16381	17263
1609	16384	17266
1610	16387	17269

Channel no	Ship transmit	Ship receive
1611	16390	17272
1612	16393	17275
1613	16396	17278
1614	16399	17281
1615	16402	17284
1616	16405	17287
1617	16408	17290
1618	16411	17293
1619	16414	17296
1619	16692.5	16816
1620	16417	17299
1621	16420	17302
1621	16693.5	16817
1622	16423	17305
1622	16694	16817.5
1623	16426	17308
1624	16429	17311
1625	16432	17314
1626	16435	17317
1627	16438	17320
1628	16441	17323
1629	16444	17326
1630	16447	17329
1631	16450	17332
1632	16453	17335
1633	16456	17338
1634	16459	17341
1635	16462	17344
1636	16465	17347
1637	16468	17350
1638	16471	17353
1639	16474	17356
1640	16477	17359
1641	16480	17362
1643	16486	17368
1647	16498	17380
1650	16420	*Distress*

Channel no	Ship transmit	Ship receive	Channel no	Ship transmit	Ship receive
1651	16528	Simplex	2219	22054	22750
1652	16531	Simplex	2220	22057	22753
1653	16534	Simplex	2221	22060	22756
1657	16711.5	16834.5	2222	22063	22759
1673	16719.5	16842.5	2223	22066	22762
1676	16721	16844	2224	22069	22765
1691	16728.5	16851.5	2225	22072	22768
1691	16554.5	17066.5	2226	22075	22771
1807	18798	19773	2227	22078	22774
1824	18882	19692.5	2228	22081	22777
1824	18850.5	19726	2228	22303	22395
			2229	22084	22780
2201	22000	22696	2230	22087	22783
2202	22003	22699	2231	22090	22786
2203	22006	22702	2232	22093	22789
2203	22285.5	22377.5	2233	22096	22792
2204	22009	22705	2234	22099	22795
2205	22012	22708	2235	22102	22798
2206	22015	22711	2236	22105	22801
2207	22018	22714	2237	22108	22804
2208	22021	22717	2238	22111	22807
2209	22024	22720	2239	22114	22810
2210	22027	22723	2240	22117	22813
2211	22030	22726	2242	22123	22819
2212	22033	22729	2246	22135	22831
2213	22036	22732	2251	22159	Simplex
2214	22039	22735	2252	22162	Simplex
2215	22042	22738	2253	22165	Simplex
2216	22045	22741	2254	22168	Simplex
2217	22048	22744	2255	22171	Simplex
2218	22051	22747	2503	25076	26151

SSB Simplex frequencies for ship to ship contacts

All transmissions are upper side band.

Code	Carrier frequency MHz		Code	Carrier frequency MHz
	2.065		12A	12.353
	2.079		12B	12.356
	2.096		12C	12.359
4A	4.125		16A	16.528
4B	4.146		16B	16.531
4C	4.149		16C	16.534
6A	6.224		22A	22.159
6B	6.227		22B	22.162
6C	6.230		22C	22.165
6D	6.516		22D	22.168
			22E	22.171
8A	8.294			
8B	8.297		25A	25.115

Marine VHF – channels and frequencies

Channel no		Ship transmit (MHz)	Ship receive (MHz)	Function
00		156.00	156.00	See below
	60	156.025	160.625	PO, PC
01		156.050	160.650	PO, PC
	61	156.075	160.675	PO, PC
02		156.100	160.700	PO, PC
	62	156.125	160.725	PO, PC
03		156.150	160.750	PO, PC
	63	156.175	160.775	PO, PC
04		156.200	160.800	PO, PC
	64	156.225	160.825	PO, PC
05		156.250	160.850	PO, PC
	65	156.275	160.875	PO, PC
06		156.300	Simplex	IS
	66	156.325	160.925	PO, PC
07		156.350	160.950	PO, PC
	67	156.375	Simplex	See below
08		156.400	Simplex	IS
	68	156.425	Simplex	PO
09		156.450	Simplex	PO, IS
	69	156.475	Simplex	PO, IS
10		156.500	Simplex	PO, IS
	70	156.525	Simplex	See below
11		156.550	Simplex	PO
	71	156.575	Simplex	PO
12		156.600	Simplex	PO
	72	156.625	Simplex	IS
13		156.650	Simplex	PO, IS
	73	156.675	Simplex	PO, IS
14		156.700	Simplex	PO
	74	156.725	Simplex	PO
15		156.750	Simplex	PO, IS
	75	Channel 16 guard band 156.7625 – 156.7875		
16		156.800	Simplex	
	76	Channel 16 guard band 156.8125 – 156.8375		
17		156.850	Simplex	PO, IS

Channel no (MHz)		Ship transmit (MHz)	Ship receive	Function
	77	156.875	Simplex	IS
18		156.900	161.500	PO
	78	156.925	161.525	PO, PC
19		156.950	161.550	PO
	79	156.975	161.575	PO
20		157.000	161.600	PO
	80	157.025	161.625	See below
21		157.050	161.650 or Simplex	PO
	81	157.075	161.675	PO, PC
22		157.100	161.700	PO
	82	157.125	161.725	PO, PC
23		157.150	161.750 or Simplex	PC
	83	157.175	161.775 or Simplex	PC
24		157.200	161.800	PC
	84	157.225	161.825	PO, PC
25		157.250	161.850	PC
	85	157.275	161.875	PC
26		157.300	161.900	PC
	86	157.325	161.925	PC
27		157.350	161.950	PC
	87	157.375	161.975	PC
28		157.400	162.000	PC
	88	157.425	162.025	PC

Notes

Functions: IS = intership; PO = port operations; PC = public correspondence
Channel 70 is reserved for digital selective calling and must not be used for voice communications.
Channel 13 is used for bridge to bridge voice communications under GMDSS. Commercial vessels will normally monitor it if a danger of collision exists. This channel is one of the few that under GMDSS can be used without a preceding DSC alert on Channel 70.

Channel 6 under GMDSS is used for communications between ships and aircraft for co-ordinating search and rescue operations.
Channel 80 is an international marina channel.

Most of the above channel/frequency allocations have been adopted by all countries though there are some regional exceptions. Some examples are as follows:

United Kingdom

Channel 0 is used exclusively for communication between HM Coastguard and rescue services eg lifeboats.

Channel 67 is allocated for small craft safety and used by small craft and HM Coastguard. **Channels M** (157.850) and **M2** (161.425) are marina channels.

USA

Channel 9 is designated as a small craft calling channel to relieve the load on Channel 16.

NOAA weather channels:

Channel No	Ship receive (MHz)
WX1	162.550
WX2	162.400
WX3	162.475
WX4	162.425
WX5	162.450
WX6	162.500
WX7	162.525

Navtex stations and times of operation

All broadcasts are in NBDP, SITOR B (FEC). Mode J2B

518 kHz Navtex

Nav/met Area	Country	Coast station	Position	Range (NM)	B1	Times (UTC)					
I	Belgium	Ostende	51 11N 002 48E	150	M	0200	0600	1000	1800	2200	
				55	T	0310	0710	1110	1510	1910	2310
	Denmark		64 05N 021 51W	550	X	0350	0750	1150	1550	1950	2350
	Estonia		59 30N 024 30E	250	U	0030	0430	0830	1230	1630	2030
	Iceland		64 05N 021 51W	550	R	0250	0650	1050	1450	1850	2250
	Ireland	Valencia	51 27N 009 49W	400	W	0340	0740	1140	1540	1940	2340
		Malin Head	55 22N 007 21W	400	Q	0240	0640	1040	1440	1840	2240
	France	Niton	50 35N 001 18W	270	K	0140	0540	0940	1340	1740	2140
	Netherlands	Netherland CG	52 06N 004 15E	110	P	0230	0630	1030	1430	1830	2330
	Norway	Bodø	67 16N 014 23E	450	B	0010	0410	0810	1210	1610	2010
		Rogaland	58 48N 005 34E	450	L	0150	0550	0950	1350	1750	2150
		Vardø	70 22N 031 06E	450	V	0330	0730	1130	1530	1930	2330
		Svalbard	78 04N 013 38E	450	A	0000	0400	0800	1200	1600	2000
		Ørlandet	63 40N 009 33E	450	N	0210	0610	1010	1410	1810	2210
	Sweden	Bjuröklubb	64 28N 021 36E	300	H	0110	0510	0910	1310	1710	2110
		Gislövshammar	55 29N 014 19E	300	J	0130	0530	0930	1330	1730	2130
		Grimeton	57 06N 012 23E	300	D	0030	0430	0830	1230	1630	2030

Nav/met Area	Country	Coast station	Position		Range (NM)	B1	Times (UTC)					
	United Kingdom	Cullercoats	55 02N	001 26W	270	G	0100	0500	0900	1300	1700	2100
		Portpatrick	54 51N	005 07W	270	O	0220	0620	1020	1420	1820	2220
		Niton	50 35N	001 18W	270	S	0300	0700	1100	1500	1900	2300
II	France	Cross Corsen	48 28N	005 03E	300	A	0000	0400	1800	1200	1600	2000
	Morocco	Casablanca	33 36N	007 38W	180	M	0200	0600	1000	1400	1800	2200
	Portugal	Horta	38 32N	028 38W	640	F	0050	0450	0850	1250	1650	2050
		Monsanto	38 44N	009 11W	530	R	0250	0650	1050	1450	1850	2250
	Spain	Coruña	43 21N	008 27W	400	D	0030	0430	0830	1230	1630	2030
		Tarifa	36 01N	005 34W	400	G	0100	0500	0900	1300	1700	2100
		Las Palmas	28 10N	015 25W	400	I	0120	0520	0920	1320	1720	2120
III	Bulgaria	Varna	43 04N	027 46E	350	J	0130	0530	0930	1330	1730	2130
	Croatia	Split	43 30N	016 29E	85	Q	0240	0640	1040	1440	1840	2240
	Cyprus	Cypradio	35 03N	033 17E	200	M	0200	0600	1000	1400	1800	2200
	Egypt	Alexandria	31 12N	029 52E	350	N	0210	0610	1010	1410	1810	2210
	France	Cross La Garde	43 06N	005 59E	250	W	0340	0740	1340	1540	1940	2340
	Greece	Iráklion	35 20N	025 07E	280	H	0110	0510	0910	1310	1710	2110
		Kérkira	39 37N	019 55E	280	K	0140	0540	0940	1340	1740	2140
		Limnos	39 52N	025 04E	280	L	0150	0550	0950	1350	1750	2150
	Israel	Haifa	32 49N	035 00E	200	P	0020	0420	0820	1220	1620	2020
	Italy	Roma	41 37N	012 29E	320	R	0250	0650	1050	1450	1850	2250
		Augusta	37 14N	015 14E	320	S	0300	0700	1100	1500	1900	2300
		Cagliari	39 13N	009 14E	320	T	0310	0710	1110	1510	1910	2310
		Trieste	45 40N	013 46E	320	U	0320	0720	1120	1520	1920	2320

Nav/met Area	Country	Coast station	Position	Range (NM)	B1	Times (UTC)					
	Malta	Malta	35 49N 014 32E	400	O	0220	0620	1020	1420	1820	2220
	Russian Fed	Novorossiysk	44 42N 037 44E	300	A	0300	0700	1100	1500	1900	2300
	Spain	Cabo de la Nao	38 43N 000 09E	300	X	0350	0750	1150	1550	1950	2350
	Turkey	Istambul	41 04N 028 57E	300	D	0030	0430	0830	1230	1630	2030
		Samsun	41 17N 036 20E	300	E	0040	0440	0840	1240	1640	2040
		Antalya	36 53N 030 42E	300	F	0050	0450	0850	1250	1650	2050
		Izmir	38 22N 026 36E	300	I	0120	0520	0920	1320	1720	2120
	Ukraine	Mariupol	47 06N 037 33E	280	B	0100	0500	0900	1300	1700	2100
		Odessa	49 29N 030 44E	280	C	0230	0630	1030	1430	1830	2230
IV	Bermuda	Bermuda	32 22N 064 41W	280	B	0010	0410	0810	1210	1610	2010
	Canada	Rivière-au-Renard	50 11N 066 07W	300	C	0020	0420	0820	1220	1620	2020
					D	0035	0435	0835	1235	1635	2035
		Wiarton	44 20N 081 10W	300	H	0110	0510	0910	1310	1710	2110
		St John's	47 30N 052 40W	300	O	0220	0620	1020	1420	1820	2220
		Thunder Bay	48 25N 089 20W	300	P	0230	0630	1030	1430	1830	2230
		Sydney	46 10N 060 00W	300	Q	0240	0640	1040	1440	1840	2240
		Yarmouth	43 45N 066 10W	300	J	0255	0655	1055	1455	1855	2255
		Labrador	53 42N 057 01W	300	U	0320	0720	1120	1520	1920	2320
		Iqaluit	63 43N 068 33W		V	0335	0735	1135	1535	1935	2335
	Curaçao	Curaçao	21 10N 068 52W	400	X	0350	0750	1150	1550	1950	2350
	Denmark	Kook Island (Nuuk)	64 04N 052 01W	400	T	0310	0710	1110	1510	1910	2310
	Mexico	Veracruz	19 09N 096 07W	250	H	0110	0510	0910	1310	1710	2110
		Cozumel	20 16N 086 44W	250	W	0340	0740	1140	1540	1940	2340

Nav/met Area	Country	Coast station	Position		Range (NM)	B1	Times (UTC)					
							0000 / 0400 / 0800 / 1200 / 1600 / 2000					
	US	Miami	25 37N	080 23W	240	A	0000	0400	0800	1200	1600	2000
		Boston	41 43N	070 30W	200	F	0445	0845	1245	1645	2045	0045
		New Orleans	29 53N	089 57W	200	G	0300	0700	1100	1500	1900	2300
		Portsmouth	36 43N	076 00W	280	N	0130	0530	0930	1330	1730	2130
		Isabella	18 28N	067 04W	200	R	0200	0600	1000	1400	1800	2200
		Savannah	32 08N	081 42W	200	E	0040	0440	0840	1240	1640	2040
VI	Argentina	Ushuaia	54 48S	068 18W	280	M	0200	1000	1800	0600	1400	2200
		Río Gallegos	51 37S	065 03W	280	N	0210	1010	1810	0610	1410	2210
		Comodoro Rivadavia	45 51S	067 25W	280	O	0220	1020	1820	0620	1420	2220
		Bahia Blanca	38 43S	062 06W	280	P	0230	1030	1830	0630	1430	2230
		Mar del Plata	38 03S	057 32W	280	Q	0240	1040	1840	0640	1440	2240
		Buenos Aires	34 36S	058 22W	560	R	0250	1050	1850	0650	1450	2250
	Uruguay	La Paloma	34 40N	054 09W	280	F	0050	0450	0850	1250	1650	2050
VII	Namibia	Walvis Bay	23 03N	014 37E	378	B	0010	0410	0810	1210	1610	2010
	South Africa	Cape Town	33 40S	048 43E	500	C	0020	0420	0820	1220	1620	2020
		Port Elizabeth	34 02S	025 33E	500	I	0120	0520	0920	1320	1720	2120
		Durban	30 00S	031 30E	500	O	0220	0620	1020	1420	1820	2220
VIII	India	Bombay	19 05N	072 50E		G	0100	0500	0900	1300	1700	2100
		Madras	13 08N	080 10E		P	0230	0630	1030	1430	1830	2230
IX	Mauritius	Mauritius	20 10S	057 28E	400	C	0020	0420	0820	1220	1620	2020
	Bahrain	Hamala	26 09N	050 28E	300	B	0010	0410	0810	1210	1610	2010
	Egypt	Serapenum	30 28N	032 22E	200	X	0350	0750	1150	1550	1950	2350
		Kosseir	26 06N	034 17E	400	L	0330	0730	1130	1530	1930	2230

Nav/met Area	Country	Coast station	Position	Range (NM)	B1	Times (UTC)					
						0000	0400	0800	1200	1600	2000
XI	Iran	Būshehr	28 59N 050 50E	300	A	0000	0400	0800	1200	1600	2000
		Bandar Abbas	27 07N 056 04E	300	F	0050	0450	0850	1250	1650	2050
	Saudi Arabia	Jeddah	21 23N 039 10E	390	H	0705	1305	1905			
	Oman	Muscat	23 36N 058 30E	270	M	0200	0600	1000	1400	1800	2200
	Pakistan	Karachi	24 51N 067 03E	400	P	0230	0630	1030	1430	1830	2330
	China	Sanya	18 14N 109 30E	250	M	0200	0600	1000	1400	1800	2200
		Guangzhou	23 08N 113 32E	250	N	0210	0610	1010	1410	1810	2210
		Fuzhou	26 01N 119 18E	250	O	0220	0620	1020	1420	1820	2220
		Shanghai	31 08N 121 33E	250	Q	0240	0640	1040	1440	1840	2240
		Dalian	38 52N 121 31E	250	R	0250	0650	1050	1450	1850	2250
	Indonesia	Jayapura	02 31S 140 43E	300	A	0000	0400	0800	1200	1600	2000
		Ambon	03 42S 128 12E	300	B	0010	0410	0810	1210	1610	2010
		Makassar	05 06S 119 26E	300	D	0030	0430	0830	1230	1630	2030
		Jakarta	06 06S 106 54E	300	E	0040	0440	0840	1240	1640	2040
	Japan	Otaru	43 19N 140 27E	400	J	0130	0530	0930	1330	1730	2130
		Kushiro	42 57N 144 36E	400	K	0140	0540	0940	1340	1740	2140
		Yokohama	35 14N 139 55E	400	I	0120	0520	0920	1320	1720	2120
		Moji	34 01N 130 56E	400	H	0110	0510	0910	1310	1710	2110
		Naha	26 05N 127 40E	400	G	0100	0500	0900	1300	1700	2100
	Malaysia	Penang	05 26N 100 24E	350	U	0320	0720	1120	1520	1920	2320
		Mire	04 28N 114 01E	350	T	0310	0710	1110	1510	1910	2310
		Sandakan	05 54N 118 00E	350	S	0300	0700	1100	1500	1900	2300

Nav/met Area	Country	Coast station	Position	Range (NM)	B1	Times (UTC)					
	Philippines	Manila	14 35N 121 03E	320	J	0130	0530	0930	1330	1730	2130
		Puerto Princesa	19 44N 118 43E	320	I	0120	0520	0920	1320	1720	2120
		Davao	07 04N 125 36E	320	K	0140	0540	0940	1340	1740	2140
	Korea	Chukpyŏn	37 03N 129 26E	200	V	0330	0730	1130	1530	1930	2330
		P'yŏngsan	35 36N 126 29E	200	W	0340	0740	1340	1540	1940	2340
	Singapore	Singapore	01 25N 103 52E	400	C	0020	0420	0820	1220	1620	2020
	Thailand	Bangkok	13 43N 100 34E	200	F	0050	0450	0850	1250	1650	2050
	US	Guam	13 29N 144 50E	100	V	0100	0500	0900	1300	1700	2100
	Vietnam	Ho Chi Minh City	10 47N 106 40E	400	X	0350	0750	1150	1550	1950	2350
		Haiphong	20 44N 106 44E	400	W	0230	0630	1030	1430	1830	2230
		Danang	16 05N 108 13E		P	0340	0740	1140	1540	1940	2340
	Hong Kong	Hong Kong	22 13N 114 15E		L	0150	0550	0950	1350	1750	2150
XII	Canada	Prince Rupert	54 20N 130 20W	300	D	0030	0430	0830	1230	1630	2030
		Tofino	48 55N 125 35W	300	H	0110	0510	0910	1310	1710	2110
	Mexico	La Paz	24 08N 110 17W	250							
		Manzanillo	19 09N 104 18W	250							
		Salina Cruz	16 09N 195 12W	250							
	US	San Francisco	37 55N 122 44W	350	C	0400	0800	1200	1600	2000	0000
		Kodiak	57 46N 152 34W	200	J	0300	0700	1100	1500	1900	2300
		Honolulu	21 22N 158 09W	350	O	0040	0440	0840	1240	1640	2040
		Cambria	35 31N 121 03W	350	Q	0445	0845	1245	1645	2045	0045
		Astoria	46 10N 123 49W	216	W	0130	0530	0930	1330	1730	2130
		Adak	51 54N 176 39W		X						

Nav/met Area	Country	Coast station	Position	Range (NM)	B1			Times (UTC)			
XIII	Russian Fed	Kholmsk	47 02N 142 03E	300	B	0010	0410	0810	1210	1610	2010
		Murmansk	68 46N 032 58E	300	C	0020	0420	0820	1220	1620	2020
		Arkhangel'sk	64 33N 040 32E	300	F	0050	0450	0850	1250	1650	2050
		Petropavlovsk	53 00N 158 40E	300	C	0020	0420	0820	1220	1620	2020
		Astrakhan	46 18N 047 58E	250	W	0340	0740	1140	1540	1940	2340
XV	Chile	Antofagasta	23 40N 070 25W	300	A	1400	1200	2000			
					H	0000	0800	1600			
		Valparaíso	32 48S 071 29W	300	B	0410	1210	2010			
					I	0010	0810	1610			
		Talcahuano	36 42S 071 06W	300	C	0420	1220	2020			
					J	0020	0820	1620			
		Puerto Montt	41 30S 072 58W	300	D	0430	1230	2030			
					K	0030	0830	1630			
		Punta Arenas	53 09S 070 58W	300	E	0440	1240	2040			
					L	0040	0840	1640			
		Isla de Pascua	27 09S 109 25W	300	F	0450	1250	2050			
					G	0050	0850	1650			
VI	Peru	Paita	08 05S 081 07W	200	S	0300	0700	1100	1500	1900	2300
		Callao	12 03S 077 09W	200	U	0320	0720	1120	1520	1920	2320
		Mollendo	17 01S 072 01W	200	W	0340	0740	1140	1540	1940	2340

490 kHz Navtex

Nav/met Area	Country	Coast station	Position	Range (NM)	B1	Times (UTC)					
I	Iceland	Reykjavik	60 05N 021 51W	550	R	0318	0718	1118	1518	1918	2318
	United Kingdom	Cullercoats	50 02N 001 26W		U	0320	0720	1120	1520	1920	2320
		Portpatrick	54 51N 005 07W		C	0020	0420	0820	1220	1620	2020
		Niton	50 35N 001 18W		I	0120	0520	0920	1320	1720	2120
II	France	Cross Corsen	48 28N 005 03E		E	0040	0440	0840	1240	1640	2040
	Portugal	Monsanto	38 44N 009 11W	530	G	0100	0500	0900	1300	1700	2100
		Horta	38 32N 028 38W	640	J	0130	0530	0900	1330	1730	2130
		Madeira	32 38N 016 55W		M	0200	0600	1000	1400	1800	2200
III	France	Cross La Garde	43 06N 005 59E		S	0300	0700	1100	1500	1900	2300
XI	Japan	Otaru	43 19N 140 27E	400	J	0051	0451	0851	1251	1651	2051
		Kushiro	42 57N 144 36E	400	K	0108	0508	0908	1308	1708	2108
		Yokohama	35 14N 139 55E	400	I	0034	0434	0834	1234	1634	2034
		Moji	34 01N 130 56E	400	H	0017	0417	0817	1217	1617	2017
		Naha	26 05N 127 40E	400	G	0000	0400	0800	1200	1600	2000
	Korea	Chukpyŏn	37 03N 129 26E	200	J	0130	0530	0930	1330	1730	2130
		P'yŏngsan	35 36N 126 29E	200	K	0140	0540	0940	1340	1740	2140
	Vietnam	Haiphong	20 44N 106 44E	400	W	0230	0630	1030	1430	1830	2230

4 MHz Navtex

Nav/met Area	Country	Coast station	Position	Range (NM)	B1	Times (UTC)					
III, IX	Egypt	Serapenum	20 28N 032 22E		X	0750	1150				
IV	Mexico	Veracruz	19 09N 096 07W	250							
		Corumel	20 16N 086 44W	250							
XI	Vietnam	Haiphong	20 44N 106 44E		W	0230	0630	1030	1430	1830	2230
XII	Mexico	La Paz	24 08N 110 17W	250							
		Manzanillo	19 05N 104 18W	250							
		Salina Cruz	16 09N 095 12W	250							

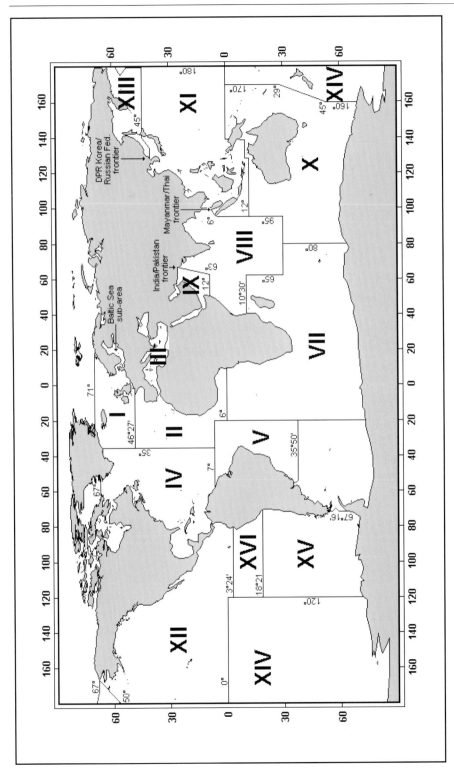

Fig A2.1 Principle NAV areas

Inmarsat-C SafetyNET™ broadcast times

Satellite	Nav area/ Met area	Product ID	Broadcast times (UTC)
AOR-W[1]	IV (NW Atlantic)	NFDHSFAT1	0430, 1030, 1630, 2230
AOR-W, POR[1]	XII (NE Pacific)	NFDHSFEP1	0545, 1145, 1745, 2345
AOR-W[1,2]	XVI (Peru Area)	MIAHSFEP3	0515, 1115, 1715, 2315
AOR-W	IV (NW Atlantic)	MIATCMAT1..5	As required, up to four times daily per active tropical storm *
AOR-W, POR	XII (NE Pacific)	MIATCMEP1..5	As required, up to four times daily per active tropical storm *
POR	XII (NE Pacific)	MIATCMCP1..5	As required, up to four times daily per active tropical storm *

[1] High Seas forecasts containing tropical storm warnings also broadcast over AOR-E
[2] High Seas forecasts containing tropical storm warnings also broadcast over POR
* Beginning 2002 Hurricane season

Inmarsat-C GMDSS equipment must be programmed to the proper Metarea/Navarea in order to receive SafetyNET broadcasts. To avoid reception of SafetyNET broadcasts for several Metareas/Navareas, Inmarsat-C GMDSS equipment must be connected to a GPS receiver or updated with a manually entered position at least every 12 hours.

MF, HF and VHF amateur frequencies

(ITU Region 1).

Band (metres)	Frequency segment (MHz)	Band (metres)	Frequency segment (MHz)
160	1.810 – 2.000	14	21.000 – 21.450
80	3.500 – 3.800	12	24.890 – 24.990
40	7.000 – 7.100	10	28.000 – 29.700
30	10.100 – 10.150	6	50.000 – 52.000
20	14.000 – 14.350	4	70.000 – 70.500
17	18.068 – 18.168	2	144.0 – 146.0

Amateur nets

Operating frequencies of amateur nets may change to avoid interference with other stations that may be operating close by. If you don't find the net you are looking for, try searching frequencies for a few kHz on either side. Operating times of nets may also change to suit seasonal variations in traffic or the commitments of those running them.

Net	Time UTC	Frequency MHz	Notes
Indian Ocean net	1115	14320	Operated from Australia
Intermar (Germany)	0700	14.313	Operates daily
Pacific Seafarer's net	0300	14.313	Covers mainly the Pacific but occasionally used by boats in all parts of the world. www.pacsea.net
South Africa net	0630 1130	14.316	Covers the Indian ocean and South Atlantic
Trans-Atlantic net	1300	21.400	Operates mainly during the North Atlantic crossing season
Tony's net (New Zealand)	2100	14.315	Daily, covering the South Pacific
Travellers' net (Australia)	0200	14.116	Covers the Indian Ocean and Australian land travellers
United Kingdom Maritime Mobile net	0800 1800	14.303 14.303	Covers the North Sea, Atlantic and Mediterranean weather

International short wave broadcasts

Listening in to news broadcasts from other countries can give you a different perspective on world events, which can be important if the political future of the country you are about to visit is uncertain. Several publishers produce worldwide listings of broadcast station schedules but these have several shortcomings, particularly for people who travel widely. First, through the use of beam antennas, broadcasts are targeted at specific regions and outside of these areas reception may be difficult or impossible. Secondly, stations change their operating times and frequencies several times a year to allow for seasonal changes in propagation and to avoid interference or deliberate jamming. For these reasons, any published listing of operating frequencies is certain to outdate quickly.

The surest way to obtain accurate broadcast schedules for any particular station is to obtain it directly from the broadcaster. At one time this meant writing a letter and getting on their schedule distribution list but now a visit to their web site is far quicker.

[Broadcaster]	[http://www.]
Channel Africa	channelafrica.org
VOA News Global news coverage	voanews.com
Voice of America	voa.gov
Rádio Nacional de Angola	rna.ao
Radio Free Asia A private non-profit news broadcaster	rfa.org
Radio Bahrain	gna.gov.bh/brtc/radio.html
Radio Vlaanderen International Belgian public radio	rvi.be
Radio Canada International	rcinet.ca
CFRB – Newstalk Radio from Toronto	cfrb.com
China Radio International	cri.com.cn
CARACOL Colombia	caracol.com.co
Radio for Peace International Costa Rica	rfpi.org
Radio Habana Cuba (RHC)	radiohc.org
Cyprus Broadcasting Corporation	cybc.com.cy
Radio Free Europe/Radio Liberty	rferl.org
Far East Broadcasting (FEBC)	febc.org
Radio France International	rfi.fr
Deutsche Welle	dw-world.de/select/0,,,00.html
Radio Budapest Hungarian Radio	kaf.radio.hu/indexa.html
Islamic Republic of Iran Broadcasting	irib.com
Israel Broadcasting Authority	israelradio.org
RAI Official Italian broadcasting agency	rai.it
Radio Japan – NHK	nhk.or.jp/nhkworld
Radio Kuwait	radiokuwait.org
The Voice of Mongolia	angelfire.com/biz/mrtv
Radio Netherlands	rnw.nl
Radio New Zealand International	rnzi.com
Radio Pakistan	radio.gov.pk
Radio Prague	radio.cz/english
The Voice of Russia	vor.ru
Radio Singapore International	rsi.com.sg/en
Radio Exterior de España	rtve.es/rne/ree
Radio Sweden International	sr.se/rs/ind_eng.html
BBC World Service	bbc.co.uk/worldservice
Vatican Radio	wrn.org/vatican-radio
Radio Jugoslavia	radioyu.org

The following bands have been allocated by the ITU for use by broadcast stations:

Frequency (MHz)	Metre band	Note
2.300 – 2.495	120	1
3.200 – 3.400	90	1
3.900 – 4.000	75	2
4.750 – 5.060	60	1
5.950 – 6.200	49	3
7.100 – 7.300	41	4
9.500 – 9.775	31	3
11.700 – 11.975	25	3
15.100 – 15.450	19	3
17.700 – 17.900	16	3
21.450 – 21.750	13	3
25.600 – 26.100	11	3

Notes

1 Tropical bands – used only in designated areas.
2 Regional band – used only in Europe and Asia.
3 Bands used worldwide.
4 Not used in the western hemisphere.

USA Family Radio channels and frequencies

Channel	Frequency	Channel	Frequency
1	462.5625	8	467.5625
2	462.5875	9	467.5875
3	462.6125	10	467.6125
4	462.6375	11	467.6375
5	462.6625	12	467.6625
6	462.6875	13	467.6875
7	462.7125	14	467.7125

3 • Technical Data

Radio transmission modes

In 1979, the World Administrative Radio Conference agreed to a designation system for radio transmissions. The following list is a selection of designations used to describe some of the more common types of transmissions.

Morse

A1A Hand Morse sent by on/off keying of the carrier

Telephony (speech)

A3E Amplitude modulation
J3E #Single side band, suppressed carrier
R3E Single side band, reduced carrier
H3E Single side band, full carrier
F3E Frequency modulation

Telex (SITOR)

F1B Direct frequency shift keying of the carrier
F2B Frequency shift keyed audio tone (FM transmitter)
J2B *Frequency shift keyed audio tone (SSB transmitter)

Data transmissions

F1D Direct frequency shift keying of carrier
F2D Frequency shift keyed audio tone (FM transmitter)
J2D Frequency shift keyed audio tone (SSB transmitter)

* Usual mode for marine radio telex.
# Usual mode for marine single side band voice traffic.

Radio time signals and solar data

Many countries transmit standard frequencies and time signals. Commonly used frequencies are 2.5MHz, 5.0MHz, 15MHz and 20MHz. Transmission format varies between stations with some extra information. Two of the most frequently used Standard time stations are WWV and WWH located at Fort Collins, Colorado USA and Kekaha-Kauai, Hawaii. Both transmit a 'ticking sound' at one second intervals. The station accuracy is better than one microsecond but due to propagation path delays, the accuracy is degraded. US users can expect accuracies to within ten milliseconds. Between whole minutes, other data broadcast by these stations includes:

- Public service announcements relating to marine storm warnings, for selected areas of the Atlantic and Pacific

- GPS information and status
- Geophysical alert information including Solar flux and Boulder K index (a measure of solar particle radiation).

This data is broadcast at 18 and 45 mins past each hour: used by software for predicting HF propagation conditions and optimum frequencies for use.

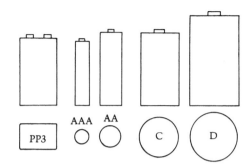

Fig A2.2 Relative dimensions of various battery types.

Battery data

Battery type cross-reference

| Volts | *ITC No | Can style | Zinc/carbon Eveready | | Alkaline | |
			Blue Seal	Silver Seal	Eveready	Duracell
1.5	LR03	AAA	–	RO3S	LR03	MN240
1.5	LR6	AA	R6B	R6S	LR6	MN1500
1.5	LR14	C	R14B	R14S	LR16	MN1400
1.5	LR20	D	R20B	R20S	LR20	MN1300
9.0	6LA61	PP3	PP3B	PP3S	6LF22	MN1604
9.0	–	PP9	–	–	–	–

*ITC – International Technical Commission.

Rechargeable nickel/cadmium cell (sintered cell) data

Nominal voltage	Discharged voltage	Can style	Nominal capacity (amp hrs)*	Maximum continuous charge*
1.25	1.0	AAA	0.18	22MA
1.25	1.0	AA	0.5	66MA
1.25	1.0	C	2.2	250MA
1.25	1.0	D	4.0	500MA
8.4	7.0	PP3	0.11	100MA
8.4	7.0	PP9	1.2	120MA

*NB These figures are for guidance only. Capacities and maximum charge rates vary between manufacturers.

Characteristics of common types of coax cable

Type	Nominal impedance (Ω)	Dia (mm)	Nominal attenuation (dB/100m)					Velocity factor	Capacitance pF/M
			50 MHz	100 MHz	200 MHz	400 MHz	1 GHz		
RG-6/U	75	6.85	4.9	6.9	10.2	14.4	19.7	78	57.2
RG-8/U	52	10.3	5.2	7.2	10.5	15.4	29.2	66	96.8
RG-9/U	51	10.67	5.2	7.2	10.5	15.4	29.2	66	98.4
RG-11/U	75	10.29	4.3	6.6	9.5	13.8	23.3	66	67.3
RG-58/U	53.5	4.95	10.2	14.8	22.3	32.8	55.8	66	93.5
RG-58A/U	50	4.95	10.8	16.1	23.9	37.7	70.5	66	101
RG-58C/U	50	4.95	10.8	16.1	23.9	37.7	70.5	66	101
RG-59/U	73	6.15	7.9	11.2	16.1	23.3	39.4	66	68.9
RG-59B/U	75	6.15	7.9	11.2	16.1	23	39.4	66	67.3
RG-62/U	93	6.04	6.2	8.9	12.5	17.7	28.5	84	44.3
RG-62B/U	93	6.15	6.6	9.5	13.8	20	36.1	84	44.3
RG-122/U	50	4.06	14.8	23	32.8	49.9	87	66	101
RG-141A/U	50	4.83	6.9	10.5	15.4	22.6	42.7	69.5	95.1
RG-142B/U	50	4.95	8.9	12.8	18.4	26.9	44.3	69.5	95.2
RG-174/U	50	2.56	21.7	29.2	39.4	57.4	98.4	66	101
RG-178B/U	50	1.83	34.4	45.9	62.3	91.9	150.9	69.5	95.1
RG-179B/U	75	2.54	27.9	32.8	41.0	52.5	78.7	69.5	64
RG-180B/U	95	3.56	15.1	18.7	24.9	35.1	55.8	69.51	49.2
RG-187A/U	75	2.66	27.9	32.8	41	52.5	78.7	69.5	64
RG-188A/U	50	2.59	31.5	37.4	46.6	54.8	101.7	69.5	95.2
RG-196A/U	50	1.93	34.4	45.9	62.3	91.9	150.9	69.5	95.2
RG-213/U	50	10.29	5.2	7.2	10.5	15.4	29.2	66	101
RG-214/U	50	10.8	5.2	7.2	10.5	15.4	29.2	66	101
RG-223/U	50	5.38	10.1	14.8	21	30.2	53.5	66	101
RG-303/U	50	4.31	6.9	10.5	15.4	22.6	42.7	69.5	95.2
RG-316/U	50	2.49	30.8	34.1	43.3	54.1	101.7	69.5	95.2
BEL 9913	50	10.29	3.0	4.6	5.9	8.5	14.8	84	78.7

The decibel (dB) scale

The decibel is a unit that is often used to describe sound levels. It turns up regularly in radio specification sheets and is often used to describe antenna gains. This versatile unit was originally introduced by telephone engineers to tackle the difficulty that, to the human ear, a sound that has twice the power of another, does not sound twice as loud. It was found that the ear has a logarithmic rather than a linear response to both sound and frequency so when comparing signal strengths it made sense to use a logarithmic rather than a linear scale.

The unit was named the bel after the inventor of the telephone, Alexander Graham Bell, and is defined as the $\log_{10}$ of the ratio of two power levels. So the difference in power between two signals, one with ten times the power of the other, is one bel (since $\log_{10}(10)$ = 1).

For most practical purposes, the bel was far too large so instead the decibel, or one tenth of a bel, was adopted and it is found that 1dB is about the smallest sound difference that the human ear can perceive. In mathematical terms this is defined as:

$$dB = 10 \times \log_{10}(P2/P1)$$

Where P1 and P2 are two signal levels to be compared and which may be measured in any convenient unit of power, such as the watt, milliwatt, megawatt, etc.

The same technique can also be used to compare voltage levels, but in this case, since power is related to the (voltage)^2, the relationship becomes:

$$dB = 2 \times 10 \times \log_{10}(V2/V1)$$

- Voltages that are halved or doubled change by 6dB.
- A voltage that is increased or decreased by a factor of 10 changes by 20dB.
- A voltage that falls by 11 per cent or rises by 12 per cent changes by 1dB.
- A power drop or gain of 10 corresponds to a 10dB difference.
- When power is halved or doubled it changes by 3dB.

Strictly speaking, the decibel is a relative unit – it compares one parameter with another. However, it is sometimes used in an absolute form where the comparison is made to a fixed level. Examples are:

dB unit	Comparison level
dBm or dBmW	1 milliwatt
DBW	1 watt
dBm(50)	1 milliwatt measured with respect to a 50 ohm load
DBV	1 volt

In acoustic engineering, the comparison is generally related to a pressure of 0.2 nanoBar at 1kHz (rms) which is the approximate threshold of audibility. Typical values for common sounds:

Sound pressure levels in dB	
130dB	Threshold of pain
120dB	Close proximity to aircraft engine
110dB	Amplified rock band
90dB	Approximate level of risk to human hearing
70dB	Heavy industry workshop
65dB	Office conversation
45dB	Home environment
30dB	Soft music
20dB	Quiet whisper
0dB	0.2nanoBar at 1kHz (rms)

4 · Further information

Book list

Admiralty Lists of Radio Signals – Small Craft NP289 Volumes 1 to 6

- Coverage includes the UK to Mediterranean (including the Azores and Canary Islands).
- Telephone and facsimile numbers for all ports and marinas.
- SSB, MF and VHF Coast Radio Stations listings.
- Weather Services including Navtex and facsimile broadcasts.
- Marine Safety Broadcasts including Navtex and SafetyNet™.
- VHF management.
- Beacons transmitting DGPS information.

Published by the Hydrographer of the Navy. This UK publication can be updated from weekly Admiralty Notices to Mariners.

GMDSS Denise Bréhaut, Adlard Coles Nautical ISBN 0-7136-6224-7

GMDSS for Small Craft Alan Clemmetsen, Fernhurst Books (1997) ISBN 1-898660-38-7

Guide to Utility Stations J Klingenfuss, Klingenfuss Publications. An annual publication giving frequencies and schedules of many different types of HF stations (except broadcast) worldwide.

The Radio Amateur's Satellite Handbook The American Radio Relay League ISBN 0-87259-658-3

Reed's VHF/DSC Handbook Sue Fletcher, Adlard Coles Nautical ISBN 0-901281-735

GMDSS Handbook John Campbell, Adlard Coles Nautical (1998) ISBN 1-84037-010-6

A Boater's Guide to VHF and GMDSS Sue Fletcher, McGraw-Hill under imprint International Marine ISBN 117 1388 028

Using PCs on Board Rob Buttress and Tim Thornton, Adlard Coles Nautical ISBN 0-7136-6210-7

World Radio TV Handbook (WRTH). Directory of International Broadcasting. An annual publication providing extensive listings of long, medium and short wave broadcast stations by frequency, time and language. WRTH Publications Limited, PO Box 290, Oxford, OX2 7FT, United Kingdom.

Internet resources

[Site]	[http://www.]
Airmail Client side software for HF e-mail	airmail2000.com
ARRL	remote.arrl.org
Black Cat Systems Multimode decoder software for the Mac	blackcatsystems.com/software/multimode.html
DX Listener's club Solar flux data and propagation predictions	dxlc.com/solar
Erik Hansen OZ2AEP Amateur radio modifications	mods.dk
FTPMail from the National Weather Service	weather.noaa.gov/pub/fax/ftpmail.txt
Globalstar mobile satellite services	globalstar.com
Inmarsat Maritime satellite communications	inmarsat.com
International Maritime Organisation	imo.org
International Telecommunication Union	itu.int/home/index.html
KB9UKD Learn to identify sounds of the various radio digital modes	kb9ukd.com/digital/
Mail-a-Sail E-mail and data compression for low bandwidth internet connections	mailasail.com
Marine Electronics Home Page A guide to marine electronics − manufacturers, dealers sites and information	marine-electronics.net
Marius Rensen's page Extensive resources for HF Weatherfax and other data modes	hffax.de/
MARS (Maritime Mobile Access Retrieval System)	www3.itu.ch/MARS
MARS Vessel callsign database	itu.int/cgi-bin/htsh/mars/mars_index.sh
MFJ Enterprises Manufacturers of tuners and other radio accessories.	mfjenterprises.com
National Institute of Standards and Technology Radio stations WWV and WWH broadcasts of standard time and other data	boulder.nist.gov/timefreq/stations/wwvb.htm

[Site]	[http://www.]
National Weather Service (USA) A huge site including much of international interest	nws.noaa.gov/
Pacific Seafarer's net An amateur radio net covering the Pacific	www.pacsea.net
Pangolin Late breaking information on this book, also YOTREPS passage reporting	pangolin.co.nz/radio/
Radio Society of Great Britain	rsgb.org.uk
RT Training Marine radio qualification and UK certificate courses	marineradio.co.uk
Southbound II Second to none weather routing service from Herb Hilgenberg	hometown.aol.com/hehilgen/myhomepage/ vacation.html
Special Communications Services Developers and manufacturers of data controllers	scs-ptc.com
Winlink Amateur radio HF e-mail service	winlink.org

Index

3rd Generation Technology (3G) 58

absorbent glass mat batteries (AGM) 70
Airmail 2000 117
amateur nets 161
amateur radio 44–53
  frequencies 160
  licences 50–3
  nets 45–6
  service 48–9
amplitude modulation 6
antennas 85–100
  heights 9
  MF/HF 88
  radiation distribution 87
  random wire 93–4
  testing 97–8
  tuners 94–6
  VHF 98–100
  whip 91
available frequencies 12–13

bandwidth 5
batteries, flooded 70
battery data 165
battery types 66–9

callsigns 15
capture effect 18
carrier signal 5, 6
cell phones 56–7
  data connections 57
  General Packet Radio Service (GPRS) 57

CEPT licences 53
channels 16–18
Citizen Band (CB) 55–6
coax cable characteristics 166
computer modes 101–15
COSPAS/SARSAT satellite details 37

data connections for cell phones 57
data reporting and polling 33
data transmissions 164
decibel scale 166–7
decoding data transmission 101–3
deep fading 12
Digital Selective Calling (DSC) 14, 24–30
distress (Mayday) 127
Distress calls 26–30
duplex channels 17

effective range 18
e-mail and internet 45–7, 116–26
  HF e-mail services 117–21
Emergency Position Indicating Radio Beacons (EPIRBs) 37–9
emergency radio service, amateur 48–9
Enhanced Group Calling (EGC) 32

Family Radio Service 56
FleetNet 32

frequencies 1–3, 160
  allocations 142
  modulation 8
FTPMail-web access by e-mail 121–3

gel cells 70
General Packet Radio Service (GPRS) 57
geomagnetic effects 12
Globalstar 59–61
Globe Wireless 120
GMDSS 14–15, 22–43
  coverage areas 23
  Digital Selective Calling (DSC) 24
  ship to ship calls 42
  strengths and weaknesses 41–2

half wave dipole 89–90
ham radio 44–53
hardware data controllers 112–15
HF e-mail services 117–21
HF operator certificates 14
HF transceiver installation 82

Inmarsat Fleet F77 & F55 63
Inmarsat Fleet F77 34
Inmarsat Mini-M 62–3
Inmarsat satellite communications 30–4
Inmarsat-C 30–3
Inmarsat-C SafetyNET broadcast times 160

international Q codes 134–6
international shortwave
    broadcasts 161–3
internet and e-mail connection
    methods 64
internet resources 169–70
ionised layers within the
    atmosphere 11
ionosphere 9
ionospheric layering 10–12
Iridium satellite system 61–2

layering 10–12
lead acid battery comparison 71
licence, amateur 50–3
licensing requirements 14
lightning, protection against 82

marine weather, reporting
    130–1
MarineNet 120
Maritime Mobile Service
    Identifiers (MMSI) 15, 25,
    138–41
Maritime Mobile Access Retrieval
    System (MARS) 16
MF and HF radio equipment
    19–21
MF operator certificates 14
MF, HF & VHF amateur
    frequencies 160
MF/HF – SSB channels and
    frequencies 142–5
mobile satellite communications
    59
modulation 4–8
    amplitude 6
    frequency 8
morse code 50–1, 133–4

Narrow Band Direct Printing
    (NBDP) telex 41
Navtex 34-6, 107–9
    stations 150–9

Ni/cd batteries 68

phone patches 45
phonetic alphabet 132
power supplies 66–75
primary battery cells 66–7
propagation of different
    frequencies 9–13
propagation prediction software
    13

radio
    equipment conformity
        requirements 16
    installation 66–84
    interference 75–82
    spectrum 3–4
    time signals and solar data
        164
random wire antennas 93–4
range 13
refraction of high frequency
    radio waves 10
regulators and invertors, battery
    74–5
requesting assistance 128
RST code 138

safety signals 127–8
SafetyNet 33
Sailmail 118
salvage agreement 129
satellite tracking, Iridium 62
Search and Rescue Radar
    Transponders (SARTs) 39
secondary battery cells 67–9
Selcall numbers 15
semi-duplex 17
ship radio licence 15–16
simplex channels 17
single side band (SSB) 7–8
skip zone 10
Slow Scan Television (SSTV) 45,
    106

software decoders 104–112
software, propagation prediction
    13
spectrum, radio 3–4
SSB Simplex frequencies 146
sun radiation 9
sunspots 9

technical data 164–7
telex 164
    codes 137
Telex on Radio (TOR) codes
    109–12
third party traffic 46
TOR (Telex on Radio) codes
    109–12
tuners, antenna 94–6

Universal Mobile
    Telecommunications System
    (UMTS) 58
urgency (Pan Pan) 127

VHF
    antennas 98–100
    channels and frequencies
        147–9
    operator certificates 14
    radio equipment 16–18
    range 9
    sets 40–1
voltage compatibility 73

wave terminology 3
wavelengths 1–3
Weatherfax 104–6
whip antennas 91 2
Winlink 119

YOTREPS 123–6